# Television and Popular Culture in India

# Television and Popular Culture in India

## A Study of the *Mahabharat*

**ANANDA MITRA**

**Sage Publications**
*New Delhi/Thousand Oaks/London*

*Dedicated to my family, in the loosest sense of the term.*

*First published in 1993 by*
**Sage Publications India Pvt Ltd**
M-32, Greater Kailash Market-I
New Delhi 110 048

**Sage Publications Inc** 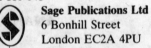 **Sage Publications Ltd**
2455 Teller Road 6 Bonhill Street
Thousand Oaks, California 91320 London EC2A 4PU

Published by Tejeshwar Singh for Sage Publications India Pvt Ltd, phototypeset by Pagewell Photosetters, Pondicherry and printed at Chaman Enterprises, Delhi.

**Library of Congress Cataloging-in-Publication Data**

Mitra, Ananda, 1960–
    Television and popular culture in India: a study of the Mahabharat / Ananda Mitra.
        p.    cm.
    Includes bibliographical references and index.
    1. Television broadcasting—India. 2. Television serials—India. I. Title.
HE8700.9.I5M58   306.23′45′0954—dc20    1993    93–27379

**ISBN**: 0–8039–9134–7 (US-hbk)
        0–8039–9135–5 (US-pbk)
        81–7036–362–4 (India-hbk)
        81–7036–363–2 (India-pbk)

# Contents

# Preface

**This work has** been inspired by the need to answer a relatively simple question about India. I was always interested in trying to find out what was 'going on' with television in India. Having grown up with the medium, seeing it arrive in Calcutta during the 1971 cricket Test match, and then watching its growth in the country, I was always intrigued by the relatively unplanned and ad hoc nature of the growth of the medium.

After leaving India, therefore gaining the opportunity to look at India from the 'outside,' and with the added advantage of exposure to the method of cultural analysis, I found renewed vigor to reexamine the medium in India. Needless to say, between 1984 (when I left India) and 1989 (when I started to reexamine the medium), television in India had changed dramatically. Clearly, the most notable change which had swept across the country and occupied a sizeable chunk of air time was the introduction of commercial serialized programs. Among these serialized programs, clearly the most popular was *Mahabharat*. India came to a standstill every Sunday morning when *Mahabharat* was broadcast. It far exceeded the popularity of any other single program in India. This, naturally, drew me to reexamine this program in depth and, gradually, I realized that to understand Indian television, one needs to understand *Mahabharat* and all it represents.

Simultaneously, another trend of events in India started, which begged attention. Television and popular culture seemed closely connected. There was an increasing projection of a Hindu macho image, and fanaticism which swept across the country, bringing in its wake miserable violence and threatening the very integrity of India as a secular and united nation. Working through the perspective of cultural studies, I saw clearly that the position of television in India, particularly the program *Mahabharat*, needed to be related to the questions of religion and nationhood in India.

All these factors led to this work. Yet, in writing this study I could not escape from my own ideological convictions as a Bengali Indian, a non-Hindi speaking Hindu, educated in the tradition of post-colonial English-medium education, and then transplanted to America, working within a European tradition of cultural studies, attempting to rethink Indian popular culture! The consequent contradictions in me haunt this project, and even as I stare at the obvious Hindu message of *Mahabharat*, a voice in me asks, 'Is that all that bad?'

However, this study reviews that precise question and reexamines the state of television in India. It then rethinks where Doordarshan, the state owned television system in India, stands with respect to India, the nation.

# Acknowledgments

This research is the result of my long-standing relationship with Dr James Hay, of the Department of Speech Communication at the University of Illinois. Since the summer of 1987, he has provided encouragement and guidance for my work on the complex questions of popular culture and television and India. Dr Larry Grossberg and Dr Ellen Wartella provided theories, texts and years of teaching and explanation which helped me to discipline my thinking and frame my research within the larger body of cultural studies. Thanks are due to the faculty, staff and fellow students of the Department of Speech Communication at the University of Illinois, whose support made this work possible.

A modified version of Chapter 6 appeared in *Media Asia*, vol. 20, no. 1, 1993.

I would also like to thank the staff at the Survey Research Laboratory of the University of Illinois, who provided encouragement during the long and strenuous period of writing. Special thanks are due to Bernita Rusk, who helped with computer intricacies.

This work would not have been possible without the support of my father, who provided me with hundreds of newspaper and magazine clippings over the five years of my research. These clippings, which were sure to arrive every week in the mail from India, make up the backbone of the secondary text that has been used in this research. My mother provided the spiritual encouragement needed in a work such as this.

I would like to thank my wife Swati for the patience with which she tolerated the late nights and the long hours that went into this research. Her encouragement provided me the hope that was so important in making this work possible. I would also like to thank all my friends and the Indian community in Champaign-Urbana whose comments and ideas made me constantly rethink my position on India and Indian television.

Finally, I would like to again thank my graduate advisor, Dr James Hay, for his invaluable guidance and my father, Dr Kalyan Mitra, for his constant support through the years it took to produce this work.

# 1

# Introduction and History of Doordarshan

*Key word: Doordarshan (distant vision), the name given to television in India*

*From a whole possible area of past and present, in a particular culture, certain meanings and practices are selected for emphasis and certain other meanings and practices are neglected or excluded.*

**Raymond Williams**, *Marxism and Literature*

## The Development of Television in India

**Television in India** is now over thirty years old. In the past three decades, television in India has experienced considerable changes, which have been examined by researchers in many different ways. This study is a textual analysis to investigate a set of television genres on Indian television, and to reach some conclusions about the role that television can play in the broad cultural, social and political map of India. Various developments in India and Indian television make it useful to engage in this enterprise, and answer a set of questions that emerge out of a review of the history of television and television research in India. The motivation to ask questions, and find possible answers, lies in the historical conjunction of a series of events focused around the development and state of

Indian television today, and its present and potential relationship with a set of other elements in the Indian scenario.

As a first step, it is useful to briefly recapitulate the stages of development of television in India. At independence, the Prime Minister, Jawaharlal Nehru, placed the development of television as a crucial issue on the national agenda. Following this, the growth of television in India can be traced along two axes. First, there were technological innovations that made experimental television possible, ultimately leading to the current form of broadcast that includes a combination of satellite connections, microwave links and color broadcast. Simultaneously, there were refinements in the variety of programs on television as it graduated from an educational medium of limited time to one that now includes a large range of programs. In this process of development, there were two issues that were the focus of ongoing debate. The first was the concern that the arrival of commercials on television would make television a medium of entertainment rather than education and, secondly, the constant tension to relieve Doordarshan of direct government control and provide a sense of autonomy to the broadcast institution. It is around these four primary areas that I have organized the discussion of the development of television in India (see Table 1.1).

## The Early Years: 1959 to 1971

Experiments with television began in India as early as 1959. To start with, the scope of programs was restricted to educational broadcasts for a limited area around New Delhi. The programs were primarily meant for medium and high school students, and were beamed at publicly funded schools in and around New Delhi which were provided with television receivers in classrooms. The principal goal of these programs was to supplement classroom-based education. In addition, there were some programs meant for farmers in the agricultural areas around the capital. These programs offered instruction on farming methods, notes on hygiene, methods of family planning and similar instructional fare. There were also some 'entertainment' programs to supplement these broadcasts which were primarily based on Hindi feature films. The variety of programs was limited.

This was the point in Indian history when the country was struggling to achieve self-sufficiency in food production, to establish

*Table 1.1: The Development of Television in India: 1960–90*

| Time Period | Programs | Production/ Technology | Control | Advertising |
|---|---|---|---|---|
| 1959–71 | Educational; some non-educational, mostly feature film based; some sports and foreign comedies; news. | Limited access, regional broadcast, black and white, some experiments with satellite and microwave links, mostly community receivers. | Government control, no question of autonomy. | None |
| 1972–82 | Same as 1960–72, with additional entertainment programs produced for television; more talk shows, quiz programs, news reviews. | Boom in broadcast facilities, experiments with color transmission. Boom in private ownership of television receivers. | Government control, some initial debate about autonomy, funded by the government. | Appearance of advertising stills. Some amount of sponsoring by private agencies. |
| 1983–onwards | Increase in entertainment programs, mostly in the form of serials, soap operas and programs specifically made for television. Large variety of serials. Increased duration of transmission with 'Breakfast TV,' afternoon programs and longer evening transmissions. Emergence of 'TV Guide,' and so on. | Color transmission is standardized. Almost the entire country brought under TV umbrella. | Increased debates on autonomy, introduction of Prasar Bharati Bill. Increased sponsorship and the consequent intake of funds. | Most serials and entertainment programs are sponsored. Increased advertising, with time slots reserved for advertising. Major sponsored programs such as *Buniyaad*, *Ramayan* and *Mahabharat*. Increased interest in audience ratings. |

a public and well-distributed primary education system, and to develop a comprehensive family planning program to stem the population explosion. Within this historic juncture, the role of television was to assist in these endeavors rather than to provide a popular cultural forum for entertainment. The usefulness of television was in its ability to reach a large number of people from a centralized classroom. The potential of television as a significant popular cultural artefact was ignored and not necessarily addressed in the discussions about television.

The production and transmission facility was based in New Delhi. It was a part of the existing radio transmission center to All India Radio. At that time the 500-watt transmitter operated in the evenings for one hour on Tuesday and Friday. Since transmission technology was still new in India, and because most of the receiving sets were located in community centers, television viewing remained primarily a community affair with specific instructional aims. These community receiving facilities were set up in places such as village halls, where public gatherings and discussions were organized even prior to the arrival of television. Television, at this initial phase, was not considered to be a medium of entertainment but primarily a pedagogic tool. Given this principal purpose of television, the institution was also financially supported by the government.

The government provided the necessary funds to maintain these experimental broadcasts. Not only did the government, through the Ministry of Information and Broadcasting, determine what was to be put on the air, but they also sponsored the production of programs and the running of studios. Most of the community television receivers were also provided by the government, and television remained very much under state control. There was little reason for any private group to consider television as a possible business venture. This is because the government, through the reports of the Chanda Commission, made it clear that television was to be a medium of education and any other programs were relatively unimportant within the future plans of television. Consequently, there was little debate about ownership, and the question of autonomy was not primary. The forty minute transmissions were sponsored by the government, and the studio was operated by a handful of engineers who were also program developers, directors and camera operators. By the middle of 1965, broadcasts had been expanded to a daily one hour program. The material of broadcast was still primarily instructional fare. However, the variety of the instructional medium had increased. There were now more programs for school children; for instance, science education for middle school children was adapted for transmission of the fundamental concepts of physics, chemistry and mathematics. Similarly, agricultural programs were longer and covered a larger range of concerns. Television was beginning to be considered a useful tool for information for the large community of farmers, particularly in the regions around New Delhi.

In the latter part of the sixties, there were rapid developments in the television infrastructure in India with the building of a spacious auditorium as an annexe to the Broadcasting House of All India Radio (Akashvani Bhawan) in New Delhi. By 1972, the Delhi center was telecasting every evening between 6:30 and 10:30. The programs were a mix of educational material and items based on feature films. Moreover, television receiver technology was being indigenously developed and an increasing number of domestically built black-and-white sets were available in the market. This led to the acquisition of personal sets, and the earlier practice of community viewing was increasingly replaced by the growing popularity of the television set among upper and upper-middle class households in Delhi. The significance of this becomes evident later, as the programs on television began to incorporate items that would appeal both to the rural farmer as well as the urban viewer in Delhi. This was, however, no easy task, and this, in turn, led to the contradiction between television programming for rural and urban India.[1] I do not believe that this contradiction has ever been resolved, but it implicated the development of the medium in India. These changes in the audience of television led to a large number of changes in the nature of television in the ten years between the early seventies and eighties.

## The Middle Years: 1972 to 1982

The period between 1972 and 1982 saw the rapid expansion of television in India. Two aspects of television that saw dramatic changes in this decade were the proliferation of genres of programs on television and rapid developments in production and transmission

[1] An elaborate discussion of this follows later in this chapter.

technologies. The educational fare of the sixties was increasingly supplemented by a large variety of other programs. These included sports, news, feature film based music programs, television plays made for Doordarshan, foreign comedies, and a large number of programs that were produced for television by people who worked primarily in the medium of television. Earlier, programs were produced primarily by people trained in the media of cinema and radio, but now, more and more people trained in television were involved in production. All this did not, however, replace the existing educational programs for school children and farmers, but supplemented them, and often reproduced them in more attractive ways. For instance, head-and-shoulder lectures on family planning were replaced by talk shows, where a set of guests and a host would discuss various aspects of birth control. In a similar spirit, quiz programs began to present educational information in the form of competitive quizzes which not only entertained but also educated. There was, thus, a shift in the nature of television, as its didactic image was supplemented by the image of a medium which would bring home the live broadcast of a cricket Test match or offer the luxury of watching Hindi and regional films in one's living room.

The significance of these developments was in the generic richness of the emerging program structure on television. What was initially an educational medium with a set of standardized programs, with head-and-shoulder lectures on a variety of subjects, was replaced with the more imaginative use of talent to present similar material in more attractive formats. This included the emergence of programs such as talk shows, quizzes and dramatizations, that would address issues of education and family planning but would do so in a way that was more specific to the narrative, representational style of television. This progress is partly attributable to the maturity of the medium, as producers became more familiar with the potential of television by experimentation, as well by borrowing the styles of foreign television. Consequently, the range of programs was expanding as the limits of possibility were tested. A good example of this can be found in geography lessons for children. What was initially a lecture was now a presentation where children participated in the program by answering a set of quiz questions about Indian and World geography, not only making the presentation more popular but educating the viewing audience too.

Simultaneously, there were great advancements in the production and distribution technologies of television. There was an increase in the number of broadcast facilities as local television stations were set up in most metropolitan areas. There was also a proliferation of repeater stations, bringing even small towns under the umbrella of local broadcast facilities. Indeed, television was producing a new geography of India, with yet another axis of difference: those who had access to television and those who did not. Although, within the next decade, most of India was brought under the umbrella of television, there was a point when there were large parts of India that could not have access to the medium. Interestingly, the Indian government was quick to realize that in certain parts of India, such as Punjab and West Bengal (which were border states with Pakistan and Bangladesh respectively), there was competition between Indian and foreign broadcasts. It was, thus no accident that the two metropolitan areas that were first to have local broadcast facilities were Jalandhar in Punjab and Calcutta in West Bengal.

There was also a rapid growth in the indigenous manufacture of receivers. This was an area that was also regulated by the government in the sixties but, with the increasing liberalization of licensing regulations, there was a boom in the commercial manufacture of television sets, and these were marketed primarily to the urban audience who were often the only ones who could afford to own them. One consequence of this expansion of the urban audience base was the recognition by the business houses in India that television was an excellent medium for advertising. This realization, coupled with the fact that the government-owned television agency was always in need of money for its expansion, led to the initial moves toward the commercialization of television programs in India.[2] This began in the latter part of the seventies and

---

[2] The term 'commercialization' is often used in quite a general sense with reference to Indian television. It is important to bear in mind that television is owned by the government in India. Consequently, unlike America, television is not a commercial venture to make a profit in the market place. However, to maintain the services and to continue with expansion, there is a constant need for funds and, initially, these funds were available through the licensing of receivers and government subsidies within the Five Year Plans. However, 'commercialization,' by the sale of air time to commercial agencies, offered a symbiotic relationship where the commercial firm could advertise their products to the large television audience and the government could earn a certain amount of revenue for offering the commercial firm this privilege. Thus commercialization of television in India does not mean that television is owned and operated by a commercial firm, but that certain businesses who can afford to, and are willing to pay a price, can have limited access to the air waves.

the early eighties. Initially, commercialization was limited to companies buying time from the government to air stills between programs.

Simultaneously, television had become a common household artefact. Most middle class urban homes were able to afford one television set per household, and television began to play a central role in redefining domestic space and time. Given the centrality of the medium in the Indian household, it was often the focus of attention in the evenings when daily transmissions would take place.[3] Family viewing of television as a leisure activity became increasingly popular.

The significant aspects of these changes were in the proliferation and availability of telecasts across most of the country; the diversity of programs on television leading to the possibility of identifying similar and conflicting sets of programs; the introduction of commercials on television; and the emergence of a variety of secondary texts that discussed the television text, for instance magazines such as *TV and Video World* that appeared in the early 1980s, 'TV guides' in daily newspapers, and reviews of television programs. These trends, along with the increasing presence of entertainment programs and the developments in both broadcast and receiving technology, brought dramatic changes to the state of television in the period following 1982.

### Doordarshan from 1983 Onwards

Following 1982, and the ASIAD games, television in India developed as a medium whose earlier 'educational' purpose and programming was increasingly supplemented by the growing presence of non-educational programs. This corpus of programs diversified from the earlier dependance on feature-film-based programs into television plays and the emergence of serials and soap operas. By 1984–85, there was a rich variety of programs in India. Some of the earlier genres (such as informative talk shows, quiz programs, educational and entertainment programs for children, feature-film-based music programs and sports programs) were retained.

---

[3] This is discussed in greater detail later in this study.

But, supplementing these, there emerged a large range of programs that included serialized narratives, soap operas, news reviews, teleplays, and a greater variety of educational programming.

For example, in 1987, the 'What's on TV' section of the March issue of *TV and Video World* described 11 different 'English and Hindi serials from Doordarshan'. These included *Sara Jahan Hamara*, a program that tells the story of '13 lovable, generous and impressible "brats" who set about tackling life on their own terms in an orphanage'; *Khoj*, a story about a lady detective; *Mickey and Donald*, the cartoon series; *Kashmakash*, which features 13 short stories all by Indian women writers; *Swayam Siddha*, which traces the story of a woman from a 'vulnerable, confused and unsure person' to a confident woman; *Subah*, which engages in the debates surrounding the quality of contemporary college life in India; *Ek Kahani*, about a set of villagers who struggle with oppressive landowners; *Buniyaad*, the so-called Indian *Dallas; That's Cricket*, which is a commentary on cricket in India and abroad; *Contact*, a quiz program for school children, and *Ramayan*, the religious soap opera. This illustrates the diversification of program types and the consequent enrichment of the television texts.

One consequence of this diversity was the emergence of a television flow, as the evening broadcast comprised a stringing together of a large number of programs of different kinds, interspersed with commercials. This differed greatly from the earlier arbitrary juxtaposition of educational broadcasts. The variety of genres now followed each other in specific patterns beginning with the early evening children's programs, moving on to programming for women and youth, followed by news and then a string of serialized programs that occupied the so-called 'prime time' of Indian television broadcast—which was initially from eight in the evening till ten at night. Given the fact that India has only one time zone, there was no question of staggering programs or having different sets of programs in different regions. The National Network went on the air around eight in the evening with the Hindi news indicating the beginning of prime time. Through these generic expansions, the development of a recognizable flow, and the emergence of specific programs such as the *Ramayan* and the *Mahabharat*, Doordarshan developed its own set of cultural and signifying practices that were specific to television in India. This was made up of program variety and scheduling.

In most parts of India, the broadcast was broadly divided between the material coming from the local transmitting station and the National Network programs originating in Delhi. This established a conflicting relationship between the regional broadcasts and the centralized national broadcasts. A majority of the serials were a part of the National Network. Further, the broadcasts from Delhi were primarily in Hindi. The regional stations carried the local language broadcasts. Also, there was only one channel of broadcast where the time was shared between the regional and National transmissions.

The duration of broadcasts were constantly increasing. By early 1989, there were three large segments of broadcasts on weekdays and Saturdays. Typically, there was an hour long broadcast in the morning starting at seven. The programs included a news section, which contained a brief weather report and forecast. In addition, there were a series of public service announcements, short skits, a couple of songs and a closing brief news segment. This was a part of the National Network. The second series of broadcasts were in the afternoon, starting around one and continuing till about four. These were primarily educational broadcasts of the National Network. Finally, there was the evening broadcast which lasted till about eleven at night. This period was divided into two segments— the regional broadcasts and the National Network. The regional broadcasts preceded the National Network which began around eight with the Hindi news followed by the evening's fare. Commercials were interspersed across the evening. However, commercials were always placed between programs and did not interrupt any program.

On Sundays, however, there was a different format. A longer morning broadcast was followed by an afternoon non-educational broadcast and then the evening's mixture of regional and National broadcasts. At the time, *Mahabharat* was telecast on Sunday mornings at nine. As on weekdays, the morning telecast began at seven with the news and a couple of short half-hour serials, followed by the *Mahabharat*. On Sundays, the broadcasts continued through the day, with a regional film in the afternoon, followed by a Hindi feature film around six in the evening and some serials and news analysis (such as *Focus*) programs until about eleven at night.

There is no real significance of Sunday within India's popular culture, except that it is the only full holiday for most offices and businesses. By and large, Indian businesses still maintain a six day week, with Saturday being a working day. Moreover, Sunday is not a religious holiday in India, except for the Christians. Thus the choice of Sunday as the day for broadcasting *Mahabharat* was primarily because it is a holiday, and most of the household members are at home in the morning. Further, *Mahabharat* filled the slot left vacant by the earlier religious program *Ramayan*. It is this Sunday morning time slot that *Mahabharat* occupied across all the ninety-three episodes that spanned nearly one and a half years.

It is also during this period that there was a proliferation of both transmission and receiving technology in India. The key developments followed the ASIAD games which were broadcast in color, using a variety of microwave and satellite links to reach a large part of the nation. This was the beginning of the expansion of television's coverage, and most of the country was soon brought under the umbrella of the National Network that carried the bulk of television programs in India. Increasingly, the programs were produced and broadcast in color, and there was a boom in the manufacture of color television sets. With the liberalization of import rules, more and more middle class households began to switch to color receivers.

Much of this technological boom can be attributed to the growing commercialization of Indian television in this period. With an increasing audience volume, particularly in the more affluent urban sectors, corporations flocked to sponsor television programs ranging from such epics as *Mahabharat* to one-day cricket matches. With the increasing presence of commercials, the corporations who were buying time on television began to show interest in the audience in terms of their demographic makeup and viewing habits and preferences. This also led to rudimentary television rating systems which advised the sponsors about the popularity of the program sponsored by them.

Meanwhile, the question of autonomy was reviewed, as different political parties debated the possibility of the government relinquishing its control over television. The most popular suggestion was in the form of a Bill in Parliament which proposed the establishment of an independent agency that would oversee the television system in India. While this did not mean that television would become a commercial medium controlled by private corporations, it did attempt to free television policy makers from the direct control of politicians. This is, however, one issue that has proved to be the focus of contradiction about Doordarshan, and I will examine this in greater depth later in the study.

It is within this context of an expanding television culture that I have to place the current analysis of Doordarshan. First, it is necessary to reexamine certain elements and moments in the development of television in India to illustrate the need to rethink television, as well as provide a framework within which to place the current project. For this purpose, I will consider the development of television in India in terms of selected chronological moments, or historic markers, when significant events occurred, as well as in terms of different tensions that developed around television as it expanded in India. Sometimes these tensions coalesce around specific historical events, like the ASIAD games of 1982, and at other times they are disconnected. I shall use the 1982 ASIAD as the turning point in the history of television in India.

## State Control vs Autonomy

The first tension was around the question of ownership. This took shape at independence, when India emerged as a sovereign country after the Second World War.

At the time of independence, Jawaharlal Nehru, the first Prime Minister of India, had declared that it was necessary to retain State ownership and control over the broadcast media in the interest of holding the country together. Any possibility of a privately owned autonomous media was set aside.

Later, the hegemonic advantages of a State-owned media became apparent at the time of the declaration of National Emergency by Prime Minister Indira Gandhi in June 1975. Just prior to the declaration of Emergency the nation was going through a period of intense internal turmoil, with contradictory political forces vying for power at the national and state levels. These factors offered the Indira Gandhi government a reason to declare a state of National Emergency, with the purpose of preserving peace, and returning discipline into the country. As a result of the Emergency, which lasted for nearly nineteen months, the fundamental rights of the Indian people were suspended, and strict controls were imposed on the freedom of speech and press. Since the broadcast media was government controlled, they readily succumbed to Indira Gandhi's control. In fact, the control on the broadcast media was close to abuse of the media, as one of the few observers pointed out: 'Indira Gandhi abused All India Radio and Doordarshan [television] for blatant partisan and personal ends mainly in order to crush dissent and promote personality cults' (Singh, 1975).

At the end of the nineteen month period of Emergency, when the Janata Party, under the Prime Ministership of Morarji Desai, was elected to power, there was a move towards progressive thinking. The new party appointed a 12-member commission, under the guidance of B.G. Verghese, a journalist, to examine the state of the broadcast media and offer some new directions. This commission suggested the creation of an autonomous corporation called the Prasar Bharati or the Broadcasting Corporation of India. This proposal struck a compromise between a privately owned, commercially motivated media and a government regulated and owned media. The term 'autonomy' meant that the media would be a government supervised institution with an independent board of directors who would have decision making powers. By this proposal, the media would be removed from the direct supervision of the Ministry of Information and Broadcasting. However, in March 1980, when the Bill was introduced in Parliament for the formation of the Corporation, it was turned down by the Congress Party majority. Meanwhile, a stage of political upheaval during and immediately following the Emergency deepened the conviction that ownership of the media was a treasured possession and should not be easily relinquished.

For an entire decade this, however, remained a bone of contention between the coalition of opposition parties and the ruling majority of the Congress Party. To fulfil its campaign pledges, the National Front Government introduced the Bill again in its first Parliamentary session after coming to power in January 1990. The new Minister for Information and Broadcasting promised that the Bill would be implemented by 1 January 1991. The Bill was ultimately passed with 70 amendments in March 1990.

The amended Bill promises greater autonomy for the broadcast media and relinquishes it, to some degree, from government control. There has been, in the period following January 1990, much debate about the effectivity of the Bill, and what it would be able to accomplish.[4] Although the introduction of the Bill did not immediately see any major changes in programming on television, it did open up the opportunity for structural changes in the organization of television in India, which could have an effect on the text of television and television as a cultural formation. Unfortunately, with the toppling of the National Front government in November 1990 and the setting up a new government backed by the Congress Party, the prognosis of the Bill was again called into question.

The critical point to note here is that any government, be it the Congress or the National Front, is basically unwilling to give up total control of the powerful broadcast media. Every government recognizes the effective role of television in maintaining the social-political bloc in power. During the National Emergency, Indira's government took this to its hegemonic extreme when the media was made completely ineffective by the government. Desai's party tried to liberalize it to some extent, as did the National Front, but their sincerity was always doubtful. Given the role that televison could play in the social-political-cultural map, no government is willing to completely give up control. Thus it is important that this vector be studied in depth to understand the role of television in India now.[5]

The first focus of tension is thus around the question of autonomy and state control. This unresolved matter suggests that there is an assumption that television can play a major role in India today. Clearly, the party in power recognizes this: that is, the role of television in impacting upon various aspects of Indian life, from images of the nation to images of religion, and the forging of a preferred national ideology. However, this also represents the conditions that determine the production of the various television texts. An analysis of television in India needs to constantly recognize this fundamental aspect of television: its state ownership which implicates the state of television in India today.

---

[4] The debate has been in the popular press, where different people (such as Chidananda Das Gupta in *The Telegraph*) have questioned the effectivity of the Bill as well as the extent to which the Corporation would be free of government control.

[5] The term 'vector' is being used in a specific way here. I choose to use the term for social and cultural forces that have a specific manifestation in a variety of practices. This manifestation is in a particular direction of social or cultural action. It is the combination of the magnitude of the force, and its specific direction of action, that makes the notion of vectors useful. It is distinct from a social force which is not manifest in any social or cultural action.

## Educational–Rural Television

A second source of tension around Indian television is the opposition between educational and entertainment programs and its relation with the rural–urban dichotomy in India. This contradiction had its roots in the way television was conceived in India, and the ways in which policy questions were answered by early proponents of State-Owned television. Education-via-television suggested a democratic and well distributed form of education, where television becomes a channel to disseminate the educational message to places where it is difficult to put up schools or provide teachers— mainly the rural sectors of India. This resulted in the linkage between education on television with a necessarily rural manifestation of this form of programming. The education–entertainment dipole got combined with the tensions around the rural-urban split. The connection between 'education' and 'rural' indicated that the benefits of didactic television were predominantly for the rural population, as opposed to entertainment television which was assumed to cater primarily to urban culture. Yet, this was a problematized dichotomy because entertainment programs were found to be widely popular in the rural sectors too. It is, therefore, insufficient to connect these contradictions in any one-to-one relationship. A brief review of this history illustrates the development of educational television and related academic research.

Television was introduced in 1959, when the first State sponsored experimental television broadcasts were beamed from the nation's capital—New Delhi. The biweekly, short broadcasts were primarily educational in nature, and only served a limited community within a 12–15 mile radius of the transmission tower. Herein lay the beginning of the rural-urban tension. The transmitting center was in a major urban city, but the purpose of the broadcast was to benefit the rural communities around New Delhi. The material of broadcast was tailored to suit the objective of imparting social and agricultural education (Dua, 1979). As Luthra (1986) has also pointed out, the programming included 'educative programs about health, sanitation, medical care, family planning and improved techniques of farming and agriculture.' Meanwhile, the urban-rural dichotomy was getting increasingly problematized as the education programs started to include subjects that were not only of interest to the farming community but could also be of use to school children both in the cities and villages. The split was, therefore, not an even binary one between rural-education and urban-entertainment. This indicated that television could not remain a medium that would be of interest to only a rural culture but would begin to interact with the urban culture too. This was formalized by the introduction of educational programs for children in both rural and urban schools.

The wider scope of educational television was established on 23 October 1961, with the formal setting up of the school and educational television system. Following this, a committee of experts was appointed to study the status of television in India, compare it with other countries, and propose a set of directives to chart the development of television in India. The two key theoretical positions that informed this commission were a trust in a model of communication that suggested a linear flow of messages from an organized source to an anonymous audience and, secondly, a strong commitment to developmental television as an educational artefact.

The commission, named the Chanda Commission, evaluated the work being done by the various media units of the Ministry of Information and Broadcasting. In their report, the committee submitted a study of the development of television in India and suggested some strategies for development. Among the highlights of the report were the clear educational and instructional thrusts of television. The commission concluded that television was conceived as a vehicle to help 'illuminate' the masses about issues that were key concerns of the government. A matter of crucial importance was developing better methods of crop production, and informing the farmers of these methods. In the absence of an elaborate agricultural training infrastructure, television was considered to be an ideal solution. In addition, population control through the effective diffusion of information on birth control and family planning held a top position on the agenda. The Chanda Commission proposed:

1. A daily school service for all middle and higher secondary schools;
2. In-service training for school teachers and village level workers suitably adjusted to the differing needs of each state;
3. A daily program for agricultural workers, for which all relevant information and guidance would be provided for the

rural community on agricultural matters, interspersed with light entertainment to hold the attention of the viewers;

4. A daily social education service which would include literacy lessons, programs for women, information and entertainment suitable for semi-educated and illiterate adults;

5. Programs for children (Government of India, 1966).

For the committee, the focus was on education, agriculture and the development of the rural sector. Consequently, educational television became the center around which most media research developed.

One trend of research considered the goals and targets of educational television.[6] Program variety was investigated by others like Coldevin and Amundsen (1985) who reviewed satellite communication technology in many countries. They suggested different kinds of programs that could be implemented for transmission over distance education systems. Singh (1984) studied the Open University System of distance education in Great Britain and suggested that a similar flexible higher education system could be adopted in India with the use of television networks.

Some descriptive work dealt with the development and introduction of television in India's higher education system (Reddi, 1987). Sharma (1985) conducted a study on the relevance and cost-effectiveness of the use of mass media for spreading education and the dissemination of information needed to sustain growth and technological progress in developing countries.

All the way from the sixties to the late eighties, the majority of researchers attempted to measure the effects of educational television. This illustrates a training in mainstream social psychology that had dominated media research in the West—particularly in

[6] Rehman (1979) conducted a study on the qualitative and quantitative targets set by the National Adult Education Program in India. Specifically, suggestions were made about the thorough and extensive use of educational media to train the instructors required to run the Adult Education Program. In a similar claim about adult education, Mathias (1975) emphasized targeting adult education through the use of satellite television transmissions. In his book, Chandrasekhar (1982) suggested the use of television to increase the scope of adult education. In an appendix, the author illustrated ways in which television could be used to serve the purpose of adult education. The use of television to spread environmental education had also been the subject of research (see, Sarabhai, 1985). These studies investigated the usefulness of television to spread information about environmental safety.

North America. This was a reductionist form of research, where the endeavor was to reduce the key questions to quantifiable variables, and then study the variations in these factors, ultimately establishing causal chains. Other descriptive studies dealt with the variety of educational television in the rural sector, emphasizing the connection between educational and the rural audience.

There are a few conclusions that can be drawn from the instances of research cited here. First, these studies reiterate the importance of educational television in India. The concern is with implementation, technology, program development and effects analysis. There is an implicit argument that since it is not possible to set up education facilities in every village in India, it might be simpler to put in community television viewing centers, and then transmit educational material over television, hoping that exposure will lead to learning effects. This is a Lazarsfeldian form of analysis, strongly entrenched in the social scientific approach to mass communication that was the mainstay of Western mass communication research at this time. Schramm's work on developmental mass communication in the Third World also had a significant influence, arguing for the developmental effects of educational television (Lerner and Schramm, 1967). Indian researchers often used Schramm's positions, insights and methods in developing research programs. They also used the results to advance a developmental aspect of communication in India.[7]

What went unquestioned were the underlying assumptions that informed this research. Some critiques (such as Gitlin, 1981) have indicated that this format of research worked from an administrative point of view, where there was an implicit need to work within a set of unquestioned assumptions, ask questions within those assumptions and provide an ultimate harmonious view of the processes involved. Based on strict behaviorism, it was assumed that learning and educational effects were easily measurable and independent behavioral attributes which had little linkage with other events occurring around the media. Also, there was an assumption that education via television involved only the dissemination of factual/textual information and did not include any other factors that needed to be considered. The educational effect of the message was measured only as a factor of the 'channel' of communication,

[7] Notable in this work is Verghese's (1981) analysis of development communication, and its future in India.

and not as a factor of the manner in which this channel recoded and reshaped the facts. This trend of research on television, particularly educational television, exposes the lack of a research tradition that attempts to rethink the nature of television as a cultural form with respect to its textual characteristics. What was not considered were the possible effectivity and role that the text of educational television would play in reshaping the popular culture of rural India, and the various cultural social practices with which television would interact to reform the image of television itself, and all that surrounds the medium. Even though the committee did not consider these future possibilities, in reality, television now occupies an important position within the social-cultural map of India. This is why it is important to consider television in terms of the text of television and the way in which television is read, and how particular texts—educational or otherwise—become reshaped on television, and reshape television itself.

Educational television research also reiterated the necessary linkages between villages and educational television, partly ignoring the urban manifestations of television. Yet the role of television in the urban areas remained a key issue, particularly because of the increase in entertainment programs on television—primarily directed towards the urban viewers.

## Entertainment—Urban Television

The tension between education and entertainment was established at the very start of television in 1959. Exhibiting an indecision about the format and purpose of television, the initial programs also included a fair amount of programming that was considered to be 'entertainment'. Luthra (1986) points out that soon after the experimental short broadcasts proved to be a technological success, the duration of broadcast was expanded to a ninety minute slot where 'entertainment fare, including music, dance and plays added in a large measure to the educative programs'. There was a recognition that television could not remain just a channel for education but would include entertainment, although it was always made clear that entertainment would be the second priority. This is also highlighted in the Chanda Commission of 1964 which added a last item in their recommendations calling it 'programs of entertainment'.

Quite clearly, programs for entertainment held a very low priority for the early planners. This was based on the view held by some policy makers that television entertainment necessarily portrayed low humor and exposed the seamier side of life. This is evident from the negative proclamations about entertainment, for instance, 'undoubtedly, constant exposure to television programs portraying violence, the seamy side of life and degrading characteristics of human nature have a harmful effect on impressionable minds'. Therefore, there was always an argument for 'attractive light enter-tainment in good taste' and 'using the powerful medium of television for nation-building activities'. Common apprehensions existed that television would follow a path similar to the entertainment tele-vision of the West, particularly the US. There was also a large body of research available in the West, for instance the work of Gerbner (1970), that was establishing a direct linkage between social behavior (like violence) in society and its depiction on television. Therefore, television in India tried its best to steer clear of those possibilities and underline its purely didactic purpose. The planners were convinced that 'education is the keystone to social and economic progress and should have, therefore, top priority'.

In spite of the assertion that education was primary, the strain between education and entertainment continued to increase. This was mainly due to the acquisition of better broadcasting technology, the proliferation of transmission centers and the lengthening duration of broadcasts. It was evident that more of entertainment was needed to fill up air time. Due to primitive indigenous produc-tion facilities, the source of entertainment programs remained largely in feature films and film-based programs, imported foreign programs, some appropriations from traditional mass communi-cation and sports.

By 1976, seven major cities (including Calcutta, Bombay, Madras and Jalandhar) had their own broadcasting facilities, with relay stations in various other cities. Each broadcasting center had its own programming mixture, while remaining within the program guidelines provided by the government.[8] In 1979, Delhi television had a mix of programs that included news, instructional programs

---

[8] This included a mandatory set of programs on agriculture, village life, family planning, and so on (Luthra, 1986).

for children, women, farmers and in-service people. Entertainment programs included feature films broadcast on weekends, film-based musical programs, imported serials such as *The Lucy Show* and the occasional airing of movie serials such as old Chaplin shorts. The last two programs underscore the increasing urban orientation of entertainment television. English is more readily understood by the more educated urban middle class audience. This was also the audience who were more exposed, primarily through Western cinema, to the popular culture of the West. The imported programs were closer in cultural proximity to the popular culture of educated urban India than rural India. Increasingly, there was a recognition that the imported English language programs were meant for the privileged urban audience. Imported programs included both entertainment and educational/instructional programs which came mostly from the BBC and Russian television, and occasionally from the United States Information Services and the Canadian Broadcasting Corporation—all in English.[9]

Another class of programs included quiz and literary programs. These programs attempted to bring about a marriage between entertainment and instruction by presenting a quiz program, often in English, moderated by a notable media personality. The language of broadcast usually included the local language and English. Thus, Calcutta would broadcast in Bengali and English, while Bombay would broadcast in Marathi and English. This was in keeping with the Chanda Commission recommendation that 'the language of television programs must be that which is used in a particular region'. With the expansion of the broadcast infrastructure, a richness in text also emerged. This polysemy would eventually have its effectivity in the way television would be linked with other formations within the Indian 'map'.

Simultaneously, there was also a growing awareness that television was becoming an increasingly urban phenomenon. This was partly aided by the fact that the primary transmission centers were located in urban areas, and the urban middle class population had the

---

[9] This is also when linguistic tensions began to emerge. Television was using a large amount of English language programs, thus splitting reader formations into a privileged group who could understand English well, and the others who were not as proficient in English. This linguistic split, later combined with a split around Hindi, will be the focus of discussion later in this work.

material resources to buy receivers more readily than the rural viewers. While the rural viewers were largely dependant on community television sets, urban middle class viewers watched television on personal sets in the comfort of their homes.

In summary, a set of significant points can be highlighted in the review of entertainment television. First, the text of television was getting more complex and variegated. The dichotomy between education and entertainment was blurred by quiz programs and attractively produced information programs imported from abroad. With the variety of texts on television, the potential meanings of the text were multiplying too, changing the ways in which television would become effective in the culture.

Secondly, television was becoming increasingly accessible, particularly to the affluent urban groups who could afford private receivers. This meant that television was getting incorporated within the urban audience, who were beginning to link the practice of watching television with other social, cultural and domestic activities. In this sense, television was becoming a part of domestic everyday way of life—a part of urban culture. On the other hand, in the rural sector, television viewing was still largely a community affair. Although people gathered at community centers to watch television, it was not necessarily a part of everyday domestic activity. The role of television in the village was consequently different, yet this difference was not investigated in research.

## SITE, Commercialization and Colorization
### (The Introduction of Color)

There were three events that reshaped the nature of television in India: The implementation of the Satellite Instructional Television Experiment (SITE), commercialization and the introduction of color. SITE was a program set up in conjunction with the US National Aeronautical and Space Administration (NASA). This program was made available to India, through NASA, a geostationary satellite ATS-6. The primary purpose of the project was summed up as:

> to gain experience in development, testing and management of a satellite-based instructional television system, particularly in rural areas, to demonstrate the potential of satellite in developing

countries, and to stimulate national development in India . . . to contribute to health, hygiene, and family planning, national integration, to improve agricultural practices, to contribute to general school and adult education, and improve occupational skills (Mirchandani, 1976).

This rather lengthy statement reiterates the usefulness of the satellite as an improved technology for the distribution of educational information in countries where there was an insufficient educational infrastructure. The SITE program brought several thousand villages under the beam of television; it also exposed the option of connecting the nation through a national network to transmit the same broadcast message, simultaneously, to all corners of the country. The SITE experiment also spawned a large amount of academic research.

Rahman (1974) has discussed the question of instructional program development and implementation; Danheisser (1975) has analyzed the experimental system, concentrating on issues of policy and implementation; and Block et al. (1979) have examined the implementation and management of a system like SITE.

There was some amount of descriptive research which discussed the hardware of SITE and dealt with the design and execution of a satellite-based instructional television system (Krishnamoorthy, 1975). More descriptive studies abound which deal with the different technological aspects of SITE, the contribution of NASA, and specific programs like the in-service teacher training program. In addition, some studies simply reiterated the fact that it was possible for nations like India to implement a project like SITE and use it with a large degree of success (Norwood, 1978; Mulay, 1978; Jain 1978).

Regarding program content, Mody (1978) pointed out that the SITE project was undertaken to provide non-formal education in agriculture and health, and formal education for primary school children and teachers. There was also the aim of promoting Indian culture, to create a sense of political unity among the nation's disparate linguistic groups. Mody (1979) also provided a detailed breakdown of the different kinds of programming that was made available by SITE.

In studying the effects of SITE, Agrawal (1978) illustrated the role of SITE in bringing about changes in the audience at the rural micro-level. The research encompassed several different issues such as the audience, content of the program and its effects on the levels of organization of the village. A similar focus is seen in the work of Eppan (1979), where SITE broadcasts were examined in relation to social realities and the cultural modes of behavior in three villages in south India. Shukla (1979) illustrated the effects of the program on a set of school children: the study examined the differences between school children who were exposed to SITE, and those who were not. The differences were principally in learning levels.

Considering the novelty of the situation and its experimental nature, most of the research was guided towards investigating the technological possibilities opened by SITE. The experiment has since then been referred to in other research about satellite TV (Agrawal, 1986; Chaudhuri, 1986; Coldevin and Amundsen, 1985).

There were a few implicit assumptions operating within this research. The research considered television purely as a 'channel' of communication, and did not necessarily consider ways in which television could reshape rural culture. Also, there was not much concern for the nature in which television could impinge upon the social and cultural formations within the audience in rural India. Some concern for social formations was expressed in the discussion about the seating patterns for TV viewing at community centers (Eppan, 1979). However, in general, the audience was viewed as a relatively passive entity. These exposed the same assumptions and shortcomings associated with educational television research. The significance of SITE lay in the fact that television became a national phenomenon. This was, however, taken for granted and the importance of this role of television was not addressed. The consequent implications on State ownership and hegemony were not necessarily raised. Yet the significance of SITE lies here—the way in which it exposed the power of television to reach the entire country, and therefore impact on every aspect of Indian life. SITE offered the technology for the use of the state controlled, expanded reach television medium by a social bloc to gain a position of national leadership.

While SITE technology generated a large amount of research, the second development—the slow entry of commercials on television—went relatively unnoticed by academic researchers. Before 1976, policy makers in the Ministry of Information and Broadcasting had been struggling with the question of commercialization for a while. Closely connected with the question of commercials on television was the struggle between education and entertainment, and rural and urban, which was slowly tilting towards the urban–entertainment dipole. This was leading to increasing cost to provide the entertainment, and the recognition by advertisers that television would allow them to reach the more affluent urban audience.

The argument of the government in favor of the commercialization of television was largely motivated by financial considerations. It was argued that through commercialization, television could earn adequate money to support itself, and finance its own expansion programs.[10] After examining the arguments for and against commercialization, the government introduced advertisements on television on 1 January 1976. The advertisements on television at this period were proposed as: 'slides or cardboard captions for ten-second exposure before and at the end of a program' (Dhawan, 1973). These eventually opened up the barrage of commercials that emerged during the historic 1982 ASIAD. This also meant that television would become increasingly an entertainment medium, aimed at the more affluent sectors of India—primarily in the urban areas.

In textual terms, this meant that the television text would now become more complex with the introduction of commercials. Eventually, in the nineties, what has evolved is that advertisements on television play a key role in framing the other texts of television. In addition, the text of advertisements have the potential for developing inter-textual relationships with everything else on television. These commercials, therefore, need to be incorporated into a critical analysis of Indian television.

The third question that had not been resolved till the eighties was the question of the introduction of color on television. Transmission in India was restricted to the monochromatic mode, and the question of adding color to television was never conclusively answered. In January 1980, the question of introducing color was again addressed by the newly formed Indira Gandhi government. Expansion programs for television were on the board, and one major area of expansion was the adoption of the color transmission

[10] It is important to note that the expansion program would ultimately be the expansion of entertainment programs.

facility for Indian television. As an initial proposition, it was suggested that experimental color transmissions would be conducted from Calcutta and Jalandhar in the early eighties.

The arguments for color transmission were driven by three concerns. First, on an international level, there had been a rapid transfer to color technology, thus reducing the availability of the obsolete black and white transmission and receiving technology. Secondly, other developing nations with similar per capita incomes (like Bangladesh, Sri Lanka and Pakistan) had already converted to color transmission. Finally, indigenous technology and technical knowhow were available in India for transforming to color broadcast.

However, the principal arguments against colorization centered around economics. The government was not totally confident that it would be ready to bear the capital costs and higher production costs associated with color broadcast. However, analysis also showed that colorization would draw in higher advertisement revenues, offsetting the higher production and maintenance costs. Colorization got linked to the commercialization argument. After colorization, the link between a commercial sponsorship and color technology pushed the medium further towards an entertainment bias. The textual characteristics of television changed too, due to the adaptation of color and other advanced technologies, all supported by commercial sponsor rupees.

All these related contradictory forces with specific directions of action—education vs entertainment, rural vs urban, public vs commercial, and monochromatic vs color—were linked together in the broadcast of the 1982 ASIAD games. In addition, New Delhi conducted a country-wide telecast of the live coverage of these games.

## ASIAD and After

The ASIAD is best described as the Asian Olympics with significant political implications. The ability to host this enormously expensive game marks the coming of age of a country. India vastly increased its standing among the Asian nations by successfully hosting these games. It also marked a moment of celebration for the Congress Party under Indira's leadership. The city of New Delhi was re-architectured with the construction of expensive hotels and better roads, and was given a general facelift. The expenses incurred were enormous, and this led to a large amount of resentment within the country. The argument was that India was too poor to host these games, and the sprucing up of Delhi was at the cost of the entire nation. However, some agreed with the government that India was indeed ready for the ASIAD, and hosting the games would vastly improve India's international image. Amidst much controversy, the ASIAD opened in Delhi—on Indira Gandhi's birthday. It was telecast all over the nation in full color, with financial sponsorship from major private corporations. Audiences who had access to television and were under the television umbrella were able to watch the opening ceremonies live from Delhi. The audience was, however, primarily made up of urban middle and upper class viewers who watched the ASIAD in live color in the comfort of their homes. The commercialization, colorization, entertainment-ization and the urbanization of television all took place in one stroke.

Many policy changes started to take place after the ASIAD. First, the government realized that the development of television in the nation pivoted around concerns of economics, and one huge source of revenue were the private advertisers. This led to an increasing number of commercial spots on television. The advent of commercials led to the second significant development, namely, an increase in entertainment programs. The earlier reticence for entertainment was replaced by a 'liberalization' of the policies, and more entertainment programs began to emerge. The third development was the adoption of sponsored programs where the advertisers independently produced programs for television, and the government sold time to the advertisers to air these independently produced programs. This quasi-commercialization saw the advent of a greater number of entertainment programs of several different kinds, from live sports to serialized soap operas, ranging from the Indianized *Dynasty* program to extremely powerful serials like *Ramayan* and *Mahabharat*.

Describing the post-ASIAD phase of television, Madhu Jain said that it was another country, in another time—an interesting metaphor which suggests that both television and India transformed after the games. Following the 1982 ASIAD, there was a sudden leap in television technology. As the Director General of Doordarshan said, color was just a metaphor for a switchover to high technology. In 1982 the number of television transmitters rose from 35 to 100. At present there are nearly 400 transmitters, making television available to nearly 80 per cent of the nation.

In summary, this phase of the development of Doordarshan is wrought with a set of broad contradictions around education/entertainment, state ownership and commercialization. Simultaneously, SITE and color technology exposed the potential of a technologically sophisticated telecast that could reach all parts of the country from a centralized transmission in New Delhi. In this study, these tensions provide the history that has determined the state of television in India today. These tensions will continue to implicate this study and the possible conclusions that can be made about the role of television in the culture of India.

## Doordarshan Today

The ASIAD determined some of the fundamental characteristics of the current state of television. First, television broadcasts are available across the entire nation. Secondly, the original priority of education has been supplemented by an entertainment orientation, particularly aided by the commercial sponsors. Consequently, television is now established as primarily an urban phenomenon. Third, television is accepted as a quasi-commercial medium, as the advertisers recognize television's potential of reaching the affluent urban audience of television. Fourth, television is more widespread, with a large number of people having access to television receivers. Finally, television has emerged as a popular cultural form, particularly in the urban areas, and a large number of people across the country now consider watching television a part of their everyday material practices and activities.

The accompanying textual richness of television opens up the possibility of richer analysis too. Television programs can now be subject to genre analysis and textual analysis to find the intertextual connections between the television text and the proliferating secondary texts (in the form of popular press about television). Its early didactic image has now been shed for a more variegated textual one. The text of television is now more complex, opening up a variety of meanings and connecting a large set of practices that range from the religious to those connected with gender and age. At the same time, the contradictions around the urban-rural bias, religious and ethnic preferences, and linguistic and regional inclinations have become more pronounced with the multiplication of texts and textual practices. Television in India is now ripe for critical textual analysis, the fundamental purpose of which is to demystify many of the contradictory but naturalized practices that surround television. Ideological analysis following this textual study can provide insights into an understanding of the tensions and contradictions, and the forces of domination and hegemony that are mystifying and naturalizing many of the discourses and formations as expected and unequivocal.

To a certain extent, this kind of research has been done in the area of cinema in India. Researchers such as Chidananda Das Gupta (1980, 1981), Kobita Sarkar (1975) and Sumita Chakravarty (1987) have examined the popular film culture of India, attempting to pin down the textual and generic characteristics of Indian films, primarily the ones coming out of Bombay. In most cases the conclusions are based on a textual analysis of the films, comparing them with films from other countries, and attempting to reexamine the role of Indian film in reproducing India's popular culture. As in Chakravarty's 1987 research, the questions have primarily revolved around the textual nature of a set of films. The analysis has then been extended to understand the representation of a larger set of issues in popular cinema. However, this approach has not necessarily been adapted to the study of television in India. The notion of the television text as a part of a large set of other texts has not been considered, as it has with cinema.

A critical textual analysis can incorporate the volatile cultural map where several contradictory forces constantly interact with each other, changing the 'map' of India and, consequently, changing the role and position of television too. In the twelve months between November 1989 and November 1990, India went through a tumultuous phase in its national history. In the November 1989 elections, the longstanding Congress Party under the leadership of Rajiv Gandhi (son of Indira Gandhi) was voted out of power in favor of the National Front government composed of a coalition of parties, including the Bharatiya Janata Party (BJP), a group that exhibited strong Hindu fundamentalist tendencies. Following the election, there was a growing sense of Hindu chauvinism in the country, finally escalating into a controversy over the legitimacy of a Muslim mosque in Hindi-speaking northern India. This became the center around which Hindu fundamentalism grew, finally leading to the breaking away of the BJP from the precarious National Front coalition, and the ultimate fall of the National Front government in November 1990. This culminated in the appointment of an alternative coalition government, backed by the ousted Congress party of Rajiv Gandhi.

It is within this complex scenario that my work on Indian television is located. Moreover, it is this conjunction of complex and contradictory vectors that provide the motivation to embark on the enterprise of finding the role of television in India's popular culture today. As the review of past research has indicated, there has not been much concern for television as a cultural formation in India. Yet, recently, television has become a significant part of popular culture and it is necessary to reexamine television as a cultural form, with emphasis on the text and the contradictory practices that surround television.

There is little intellectual interest in trying to explore the role of television in the production of the emerging cultural, social and national formations. This is precisely why it is important to rethink the role of television as a part of the larger popular cultural landscape.

Television, therefore, is no longer an independent didactic intervention, but a close accomplice in the production of popular culture. Within this cultural space, television is circulating several different signs, symbols and images (for instance, those of national integration, education, urbanization and consumption behavior). Yet, this process has not developed into a recognizable hegemonic order, but is still engaged in a hegemonic struggle to produce a single ideological position. The notion of struggle is evident in every aspect of Indian life and culture, and television has been doggedly involved in this struggle, constantly vying to carve a position of its own within India's popular culture. It is this element of struggle that makes it all the more important to study television as a cultural formation, and recognize the struggle that is continuing around the medium. For instance, the question of State ownership and possible autonomy of an Indian Broadcasting Corporation, contested around the controversial Bill in Parliament, represents a political manifestation of the struggle. The impact of such a struggle has repercussions in all the connected elements—from the policies around news to the way Indian audiences will relate to television.

Therefore, it becomes important to raise a series of new questions about television. The focus needs to be on a textual analysis of television to examine its emergent rich textual nature. Also, the questions need to examine the relation of television with the many elements that surround it, and the contradictions between the elements. Finally, we need to examine the role that the emergent cultural formation of television can play in India's popular culture. However, given the wide scope of analysis, it is also important to focus on only a selected number of issues and texts to keep the analysis manageable and meaningful.

## *The Question*

All these concerns converge in the question: What does a *textual analysis* of a set of *television genres on Indian television* tell us about the *role of television* in *India's popular culture*?

The first concern is with 'culture' and 'popular culture'. These are multi-discursive, and contextually specific terms which have gone through several transformations within different disciplines at different times and in different societies. Therefore, it is important, at the outset, to clarify 'culture' and 'popular culture' and point out their usage in this discussion, particularly within the framework of critical textual analysis which is a part of the wider body of research called 'cultural studies'.

Next, textual analysis is principally a question of methodology: a particular way in which one can examine texts and arrive at conclusions about the text. In this particular instance, the concern is with the television text, and finding an appropriate way to analyse it. However, this can be done after substantiating the claim that textual analysis is a reasonable way to understand texts, illustrated by past theoretical and empirical examples.

The focus on textual analysis leads to genre analysis. I will examine the various manifestations of the theory of genre in its current usage in the examination of the television text. This will provide the rationale for choosing one specific television genre on Indian television following a brief overview of the various genres that are currently identifiable on Indian television. This will result in a detailed discussion of the textual characteristics of the specific genres.

The textual analysis will then be broadened into an ideological enquiry where I will examine the relations between television and the nation, television and religion, and the role of television in relation to gender and language. All these concerns are important in the current Indian scenario which is wrought with regional separatism, religious fanaticism, uncertainties about the possibility of defining the position of women in India and the inability to find an integrated, common and acceptable language for the nation. Needless to say, all these factors are interrelated, and the goal would not be to find any universalizing tenets, but to question the current scenario, examine the contradictions, and investigate the way in which television is related with these wider concerns (for instance, those of religion, gender and language).

The next step in this direction is to understand the concept of culture and popular culture. These constructs are multi-discursive in nature, and their interpretations are closely bound to their specific discursive use. It is, therefore, important to review the various usages of the terms 'culture' and 'popular culture' and then settle on the ways in which the terms will be used in the current discourse.

# 2

# Reformulating Culture in the Indian Context

*Are we to understand 'culture' as 'the arts', as a 'system of meanings and values', or as 'a whole way of life', and how are these to be related to 'society'?*

—**Raymond Williams**, *Marxism and Literature*

## Introduction

This study, the textual analysis of a genre on Indian television, examines the position of Doordarshan in a cultural map of India: elaborating the role that Doordarshan plays in Indian culture, implicating that culture and being implicated by that culture. This enterprise involves rethinking two fundamental issues: one, culture itself and, two, the connection between culture and the variety of textual, narrative and generic practices of television.

These two issues are intimately related within a framework where culture is elaborated as the product of a combination of material practices. These practices refer to a large variety of elements, including the everyday material practices of particular social blocs at any moment in time, as well as the specific signifying practices of television. Simultaneously, it incorporates the question of ideology in its material existence in practices, ideological struggle among practices, and the consequent ideological dimension of culture.

Therefore, the claim that a textual analysis of Doordarshan will provide insights into the position of Doordarshan in the cultural map of India presupposes that culture is an ideologically produced articulation of a variety of practices, among which the representational practices of Doordarshan are a significant part. This is precisely why it is important to reconsider the notion of culture as a combination of a variety of practices that are often in conflicting relationships, pulled together by the work of ideology, and circulated by a hegemonic leadership. Following the reconsideration of culture, it will be possible to review the methods of textual and generic analysis, finally engaging in such an analysis to arrive at answers to the question posed in the earlier chapter. As a first step, I will review some of the key debates around the term 'culture' within the field of cultural studies. This not only helps to rethink the notion of culture, but also provides an overview of some of the theoretical underpinnings of 'cultural studies'—the paradigm within which this entire research is located.

## Culture as an Articulation of Practices

In order to examine the nature of culture, a possible starting point is the way in which O'Sullivan and others have described culture as: 'the institutionally or informally organized social production and reproduction of sense, meaning and consciousness' (O'Sullivan, Hartley and Saunders, 1983). They are quick to point out that the word culture is multi-discursive, its provisional meaning being determined by its specific usage within a particular discourse. However, another important aspect of their definition lies in the emphasis on sense, meaning and consciousness. These remain three aspects of culture that are recurrent in all the different ways in which culture has been discussed and debated within the area of cultural studies. In addition, their emphasis on the institutional as well as the informal has been maintained in the different ways in which culture has been discussed. It is both through informal (such as gossip) as well as institutional (such as mass media) channels that culture is produced and reproduced. One aspect that is, however, not explicitly mentioned in this description is the aspect of culture as a set of practices. However, it is through a set of material practices that surround the institutional and informal that sense, meaning and consciousness is produced and reproduced. Within the various stages of cultural studies, as pointed out by Hall (1980c), one issue that recurs is the concept of culture as a set of practices. In the Arnoldian sense of culture, it was composed of a set of practices, though elitist, but material practices of a group of people. Williams highlights this in saying that, in the classical sense, culture was also conceived as a set of practices. In his words, 'culture is a general classification of "the arts," religion, and the institutions and practices of meaning and values' (Williams, 1977).

Later, within the sociological aspect of cultural studies, particularly influenced by Williams, Hogart and Thompson, culture was removed from its traditional moorings within text and artefact and taken to the wider field of social practices. Following the next major structuralist influence of Levi-Strauss and Althusser, culture was located in the structure of dominance and emphasis shifted to cultural practice embedded in the structures of society—within its systems of domination and difference. Thus culture as a set of practices has been a key aspect in the tradition of cultural studies.

The notion of practice involves the lived experiences and activities of a group of people within specific social blocs at specific moments in history. It is important to recognize that there are a set of activities that are performed in the social and cultural arena that determine the practices of a social group. Yet this notion of practice is also the most thorny one. It is, indeed, too easy to accept that there are only a limited set of activities that are the natural practices for a social group, and attempt to describe such a limited and harmonious set of practices as the 'cultural' practices of the social group. Geertz's (1973) work on different South Asian nations attempts to find a set of practices that can be described as national practices. His treatise on the Balinese cock fight is perhaps the most popular of his writings, where he attempts to locate, within a limited set of practices, a cultural description of a particular set of people. To some extent, the question of cultural anthropology has often revolved around the identification of such practices that can, in turn, be used as central points around which to 'imagine' a nation or social group. This leaves one with the notion of practices as a harmonious set of symbolic, cultural, social and economic activities that are natural to any community of people. And when culture is theorized as a set of practices, culture itself tends to become monolithic and centralized. It is precisely here that the notion of a centralized and common culture becomes embedded and naturalized. This is problematized by the relation between culture and ideology as developed by Althusser and Gramsci, and later refined by Hall and others. By relating culture and ideology, it is possible to examine the internal contradictions within practices, as well examine the way in which ideology informs practices, thus informing culture itself. Ideology introduces in the discussion the elements of struggle, contradiction and dominance, all of which are important in studying culture as a set of practices.

Althusser refined the notion of ideology in the area of cultural studies. Using his thesis on ideology, and the Gramscian notions of hegemony and the national–popular culture, it is possible to establish the ideological nature of culture and reinforce the claim that culture is made up of a set of interrelated but often contradictory practices constantly struggling with each other. The notion of ideology has been a key aspect in the vocabulary of Marxist thinking for a long time. Initially, in the works of Marx, ideology was proposed as a sense of false consciousness, with a necessary correspondence between class and ideology, with every class having its own ideology, where the ideology of the ruling and dominant class became the ideology of the people. Within this notion of necessary correspondence, it was difficult to locate the site of struggle against such a ruling ideology. In addition, it was also difficult to identify the processes through which ideology was experienced and circulated. Using the structuralist approach towards Marxism, Althusser (1986) proposed a more elaborate description of ideology locating it in the imaginary relationships of individuals with the real conditions of existence. In addition, in the second part of the thesis on ideology, he proposed that ideology has material existence manifest in the material practices of the people. Thus the work of ideology was located within a set of material practices, therefore establishing a relationship between ideology and culture. It is, thus, a particular set of material practices that tend to become dominant and preferred through a process of hegemonic struggle.

Gramsci (1971), the Italian thinker, posits that hegemony is the process by which a ruling bloc wins a position of leadership over the rest of the people by gaining the willing consent of the subordinate blocs. Hegemonic struggle becomes a complex negotiation between the dominant and subordinate, where the dominant only needs to gain the consent of the subordinate. Hegemony also represents a constant set of struggles between the dominant and subordinate, where the dominant has to constantly struggle to maintain its position of leadership. Using the notion of hegemony, Gramsci proposes the notion of national–popular culture as the forging of a relationship between the leaders and the popular, a phenomenon that Gramsci argues did not ever happen in Italy. In other words, it can be argued that the notion of a national–popular culture requires the workings of a successfully embattled hegemonic struggle where the ruling bloc (for instance, the intellectuals in Gramsci's Italy) has been able to forge the willing consent of the popular in producing a set of practices as the national–popular cultural practices of a nation. Within this framework, and by using the argument that culture is made up of a set of practices, it is possible to claim that culture is, in fact, an ideological construct made up of a set of material practices that have been established as dominant, natural and normal through the workings of a hegemonic struggle.

Many authors have advanced these arguments about culture, and particularly popular culture, to establish that culture is made up of a set of practices, and that culture is ideological. Fiske (1987a and b) has maintained that popular culture is ideological, and is produced around a set of practices. He has argued that popular culture needs to be understood from the bottom up, as a set of practices of negotiation and meaning production, where the people produce peculiar and unique meanings out of the available artefacts of a culture industry. He has used de Certeu's notion of tactical warfare in describing the process of meaning production, claiming that it is around a set of practices of evasion and negation that popular culture is produced. Within this framework, culture remains embedded in a set of practices (Fiske, 1989).

Similarly, the works of Hebdige (1979), Paul Willis (1977) and other scholars of sub-cultural studies have maintained that the study of sub and counter cultures is located in a set of unique practices that are specific to the particular sub and counter social formations. However, this sub-cultural work also brought into question the theory of a necessary correspondence between particular social formations and their cultural practices. The body of work on youth culture in Britain and the work of Hall on Jamaican culture identified the notion of a class belongingness of culture, and questioned the assumptions that culture remained specific to classes. It is here that the notion of articulation, developed by Laclau and refined by Hall, becomes particularly generative. The key problem remained in the argument that a necessary correspondence was assumed between class position, ideology and culture. In order to surmount this deterministic and restrictive argument, it was suggested that there was, in fact, no necessary correspondence between these vectors, but there existed temporary and unnecessary connections or 'articulations' between these elements at specific moments in history. The notion of articulation becomes important in developing the discussion of culture. It is possible to argue that culture itself is also an articulation of several different elements. In order to establish this, I shall first examine the theory of articulation in some detail.

The notion of articulation is drawn from the works of Laclau, and developed principally by Hall as a theoretical principle about a non-reductionist and historical analysis of the relation between ideology, social forces and subjectivity. The term articulation in British usage has a dual meaning: on the one hand, it refers to utterances, while, on the other hand, it refers to the way in which vehicles are chained together or 'articulated' together to form a whole, with the possibility of separation, without any necessary essentiality to the connections. In a similar way, Hall proposes that various elements in society are connected together in a non-necessary way forming provisional unities and creating temporary connections which, however, are produced as natural through a process of hegemonic struggle and domination. Here the work of ideology is to produce these articulations as natural. At specific historic moments, unique connections are forged between different elements. The theory of articulation emphasizes the non-necessary nature of these connections, the lack of determinacy in these connections, the lack of anything absolute about these connections and the non-essential nature of these connections. Theoretically, this was a means to move away from the deterministic notion of necessary relationships between class position, ideology, material practices, culture and experience. Here the focus is on the notion that there are no necessary connections between these elements but, in fact, these are unities that are artificially produced and are open to question and challenge. In the words of Hall, the theory of articulation as I use it has been developed by Eernest Laclau, in his book *Politics and Ideology in Marxist Theory*. His argument there is that the political connotations of ideological elements have no necessary belongingness, and thus, we need to think of the contingent, non-necessary, connection between different practices—between ideology and social forces, and between different elements within ideology, and between different social groups composing a social movement, etc. He uses the notion of articulation to break the necessatarian and reductionist logic which has dogged the classical marxist theory of ideology (Hall, 1986a).

I have used this rather lengthy quote from Hall because it becomes the kernel of numerous future works by Hall and others to delve into the intricacies of several different social phenomenon, movements and practices, and has proved to be quite useful in epistemological value.

Hall has discussed the question of particular sub-cultures—mainly the Jamaican black in Britain—and has proposed that the social location of the sub-group is determined by the alignment and articulation of several different social vectors that ultimately over-determine the location of the sub-group within the wider socio-cultural map of Britain. He has discussed social relations in Jamaica and Britain in terms of an interdiscursive field generated by the articulation of different vectors like class, race and gender. In this sense, the theory of articulation provides a way in which to image the political and social position of particular groups.

In a similar way, the work of Gilroy (1986) about race and racism in Britain has also drawn on the notion of articulation, constantly fighting a socio-anthropological explanation of racism, and urging an understanding of race politics and racism as a process that is articulated with several other political forces and vectors, particularly those of class and gender. It is through unique connections between different elements that provisional chains of equivalence are formed that are made to look natural. This hegemonic process of producing arbitrary connections between social and cultural elements is particularly evident in the case of race politics in Britain, where a general economic slump has been articulated, or connected, by the white right, with the existence of immigrant blacks. Gilroy has argued here that this is indeed an artificial argument which has been circulated as natural and normal through a hegemonic process. In his words,

> there is no one-to-one correspondence between the 'crisis of race' and the economic crisis. Yet race is always present, whether the issue under discussion is the growth of unemployment, the role of the police in inner-city areas, or the recent race riots in a number of major cities (Solomos, Findlay, Jones and Gilroy, 1986).

This discussion of race, and the argument that race, racism and race struggle is a complex process of articulation, also opens up another key factor about the theory of articulation and its usefulness in understanding the processes and implications of struggle with a dominating system.

The fact that articulations are non-essential, and are a product of hegemonic struggles working through ideology, opens up the possibility of arguing for a field of ideological struggle through which such articulations are broken and rearticulated in new and different ways, opening up the space to accommodate the voice of the subordinate. This is precisely the task Gilroy and others are engaged in. Their key attempt has been to point out the non-essential nature of the connections and pose them as a problematic that is open to reappraisal and rearticulation. Hall has labelled this process ideological struggle because, in the end, the work of ideology is to forge the chains of equivalence, and it is through a process of ideological struggle that these chains are broken and reformed. In Hall's words:

> a particular ideological chain becomes a site of struggle not only when people try to displace, rupture or contest it by supplanting it with some wholly new alternative set of terms, but also when they interrupt the ideological field and try to transform its meaning by changing or rearticulating its associations, for example, from the negative to the positive (Hall, 1985).

Hall illustrates this process by examining how the connotations and ideological meaning of the term 'black' have shifted over time, through a series of struggles, from a connection with slavery to the more recent connection produced in the discourse 'black is beautiful'. In a similar way, most hegemonic articulations are open to struggle, and it is possible to break the chains of equivalence to produce a new set of articulations that represent a different set of unities forged through struggle. This aspect of the articulation theory is a further move away from the reductionist argument about the connection between ideology, social positions and social experiences, and a further reconfirmation of the theory that there are no necessary connections between different elements. In a similar way, culture itself is also artificially produced through hegemonic processes. Also, the way culture is produced can be changed and, through ideological struggle, the practices around culture can be redefined and reproduced. These articulations are not guaranteed either with respect to the elements it combines, or the manner in which the combination is produced. Thus culture is open to question, and the practices that produce culture are open to question and reappraisal.

Finally, by using the notion of articulation and no necessary connections, several refinements have been produced in the relations between society and culture. Working particularly from the notion of 'marxism without guarantees', Grossberg (1986) proposes a conjunctural view of society, history and subjects without attempting to find any final and closed answers. He seeks provisional chains of equivalence to use as the fulcrum of criticism and analysis. Through a conjunctural approach, Grossberg has described society as:

> a complex unity, always having multiple and contradictory determinations, always historically specific. This conjunctural view sees social formations as a concrete, historically produced organization—a 'structure in dominance'—of the different forms of social relations, practices and experiences (Grossberg, 1986).

This quote provides a very elaborate description, as well as an opportunity to pull together all the different strains that have been discussed so far. The first key contention is that society is made up of a set of contradictory forces, creating out of them social formations. Here I have abandoned any harmonious and guaranteed sense of social blocs, and have focused on the internal contradictions that make up the social blocs. Within this society, there is an interplay of practices. Social formations are organized around a set of practices that have become natural and normal for the social formation, in spite of the fact that there might be internal inconsistencies within the practices, and the fact that the practices are the product of a system of dominance that has been able to produce such practices as natural and normal. Finally, within this construct there is no sense of guaranteed determinacy but, on the contrary, there is a sense of overdetermination, where every practice influences the other and is, in turn, influenced by other practices. It is then argued that within this contradictory unity that society is, there are constant struggles for dominance. Culture, in this complexly defined society, is the articulation of a set of different practices in a provisional unity. Culture is also the site of struggle to maintain that unity and, to disarticulate the unity and forge new articulations and produce new connotations. Thus culture can be elaborated as the articulation of a large set of elements which include social relations, signifying and non-signifying practices and lived experiences.

Culture is ideological and is a product of hegemonic struggle where particular chains of equivalence between these different vectors have been produced as normal. Along with this, there is the contention that culture is neither guaranteed nor determined by any single factor, but is indeed a provisional and open horizon where there is an interplay of forces that are constantly shifting with time. In addition, culture does not remain a harmonious monolith but is overdetermined by the internal contradictions and unevenness of the social formations. Culture becomes multidiscursive and becomes the product of intersecting discursive formations where several different forces interact to produce an ideologically informed culture. This approach includes the notion of emergent and residual formations proposed by Williams (1977), where it is possible to find within the unities elements from a previous time, as well as elements that are emergent in society. Culture becomes embedded within the structures of dominance that characterize society and the network of practices and relations within which particular individuals are positioned and identified.

## *Towards a Framework of Culture in India*

Culture is thus closely tied to history, the geographic location of a social bloc, and the moment in time when culture is being studied.[1]

[1] This is precisely what O'Sullivan et al. (1983) point out in their brief description of culture in *Key Concepts*. According to the authors, the notion of culture has

In India, too, culture has been formulated in a manner specific to India, its history and its specific practices.

It is also important to note that the tradition of cultural studies emerges out of a very specific history and region of the world.[2] Within the post-War devastation of the British working class, a set of thinkers began to develop a school of criticism that was labelled cultural studies. The work of Hoggart, Thompson and Williams concentrated on the questions of culture in Britain. As pointed out earlier, this work was then elaborated by other scholars. They were able to identify some fundamental assumptions about culture that are applicable to other histories and social blocs. Even though culture remains bound to the histories and geographies of regions of the world, there are often similarities in the way in which culture is conceptualized that offer the space to ask similar questions about culture, albeit in different settings.

In the case of India, the traditional elitist sense of high culture offers that space of questions. And the questions, I would argue, are best framed within the tradition of cultural studies. This is precisely because scholars of cultural studies were interested in examining the elitist notion of culture in Europe, particularly in Britain.[3] Although the practices that made up the culture of post-War Britain are different from those in India, the cultural studies tradition opens up the space to question the traditional moorings of culture and rethink the concept of culture as the articulation of everyday life material practices. This is precisely why the tradition of cultural studies offers generative ways of rethinking the traditional notion of culture in India too.

----

gone through several conceptual changes at various points in time. They point out that the term is multi-discursive and can be mobilized in different ways in different discourses.

[2] Hoggart points to this in his treatise on contemporary cultural studies in Britain in saying, 'It is to stress that the shape and pressure of this concern (in terms of literary traditions—a key element of cultural studies) differ within different cultures' (Hoggart, 1969).

[3] Hoggart pointed out, in his approach to the study of literature and society in Britain, that the tradition of literary studies in Britain presupposed a necessary connection between 'good literature' and 'high literature'. According to him, it was only recently (he was writing in 1969), that there was a rethinking of this assumption and a move to consider alternative ways of looking at literature and art, where no a priori connection between the two is drawn.

## High Culture: Tradition, Sponsorship and Religion

Within the Indian context, the notion of culture has historically been connected with elitist and high culture.[4] Culture was related with a sense of privilege, being used synonymously with 'high' culture. The notion of high has a dual connotation: on the one hand, it is a cultural product that is superior in quality and, on the other hand, the product belongs to a social bloc that is considered superior, and has been able to seize a position of leadership. The notion of high culture thus refers not only to the finer aspects of art, literature and music, but also to a social faction that has easy access to this 'high' culture. Within this conceptualization, the term culture is synonymous with artistic achievements that are traditionally recorded by historians—temples and castles, and musical, literary and artistic masterpieces.

Indeed, in India, the notion of 'high' culture has been examined in depth, to unravel the various ways in which it developed and was perpetuated. However, there is little critique of high culture in this predominantly historical analysis. Instead, there is the assumption that Indian culture is mainly classical culture exemplified in classical dance, music and art forms.[5] Three key interrelated factors emerge in the refinement of the notion of high culture in India: culture and tradition, culture and sponsorship and culture and religion.

*Culture and Tradition:* There has always been a strong link between tradition and culture in India. In other words, culture in India has to withstand the test of time. Only those cultural expressions, forms and artefacts that have been in existence for long are considered a part of authentic Indian culture. A good example of this

---

[4] The work of Mahadev Apte (1978), John Elder (1978), David Kinsley (1982) and Narayana Menon (1986) all recognize the centrality of this elitist culture in the conceptualization of culture in India. The historical treatise of authors such as these attempt to reconsider culture within this framework.

[5] This is evident in a variety of cultural histories of India, for example, in the words of a cultural historian, Ananda Coomarswammy; 'Indian art and culture are a joint creation of the Dravidian (the earliest civilization of India, circa 5000 B.C.) and the Aryan genius, a wielding together of the symbolic and the representative, the abstract and the explicit, of language and thought' (Coomarswammy, quoted by Menon, 1986). This only emphasizes the necessary connection that is drawn between the ancient, high and Indian culture.

is Indian classical music. The very adjective 'classical' places this musical form in a timeframe that extends to around 1500 B.C.. As the sociolinguist Mahadev Apte points out,

> The claim is made that even before the end of the Vedic period (1500 B.C..) the scale of seven notes, so basic a concept in the classical music of India, was completed, and that all the tempos of the rhythms were known in the later Vedic Age (Apte, 1978).

It is this same tradition of music that is still placed within the highest strata of musical expression in India. As Apte also points out, there is always a concern among the scholars and practitioners of classical music that, with the increasing popularity of this music form, music will lose its position of stature and slip into the realm of 'low' or non-elitist culture.

It is precisely this process that is at work, for instance, in the dance form that has been called *mujra*. This is a dance which catered primarily to the tastes of the elitist male in India. The dance took place in sophisticated brothels called *kothas*, and attracted the rich and the elite. However, this is now changing and, to some critics, this change is for the worse in two respects: first, in the loss of quality of the dance form and, secondly, in the loss of 'quality' of the audience. A recent piece in *India Today* illustrates these points:

> The free wheeling dance steps are a far cry from the traditional, and the whole affair is aimed at providing nothing more than simple entertainment.
>
> Naina Devi, a connoisseur of mujra, reminisces about the famous Chawri Bazaar in Delhi that used to be lined footpath to footpath with Rolls Royces, Daimlers and the like, depositing aristocrats and the wealthy to the 'kotha' (Sawhney, March 1991).

This signifies two issues that are becoming increasingly crucial in the relationship between heritage and culture in India. First, there is still a tendency to equate culture with tradition, and the fall of a cultural practice, like the *mujra*, from this traditional pedestal is viewed with anxiety. Secondly, there is an increasing tendency to disseminate the connection between tradition and culture by questioning the authenticity of this connection and by incorporating the traditional 'high' culture practices within popular culture. Both these issues point to the need to rethink Indian culture and analyze the connection between culture and tradition. This is part of the project of cultural studies where the particular, essential, and necessary are reexamined.

The question of tradition is also connected with the issue of sponsorship. One of the reasons that a particular artefact or musical form has passed the test of time is because there was sponsorship available for the particular cultural expression.

*Culture and Sponsorship:* Traditionally, cultural expressions were sponsored either by the royalty or by religious institutions, who represented social blocs which had the economic ability to do so. For example, classical dance in India, a principle example of Indian culture, was often the product of dances in ancient Hindu temples, or dances within the royal court.[6] This is pointed out by Joseph Elder, who says:

> The rajas and the gentry of Kerala supported Kathakali dancers and dance troups . . . the cave temples, sculptures, and paintings at Ajanta, Ellora, and Elephanta were almost certainly created by artists supported by Buddhist, Jain, and Hindu organizations (Elder, 1978).

Similarly, the emergence of classical Indian music has been sponsored by the royalty too.

The significance of sponsorship is in the process of selection, where particular cultural practices would enjoy the privilege of

---

[6] In a lecture on culture, a noted scholar on Indian culture, Narayana Menon, who was the chairman of the Indian Academy of Music, Dance and Drama, explicates the richness of the Indian classical dance form. His entire thesis is a useful re-examination of the complexity and the consequent richness of classical dance, but it does not address the relationship between the dance form and the patronage that was instrumental in providing the support for the dance form to last through thousands of years. This is precisely the kind of analysis that is rare in thinking of Indian culture. Consequently, much of the significance of the relation between high culture and patronage is lost.

royal or religious sponsorship.[7] Consequently, certain other practices would be marginalized and not be given the chance to grow.
From a historical perspective, Elder points to this saying, 'Looking
at patron Culture through Indian history, one notes a not-so-
surprising association between patrons investing money in the arts,
and the flourishing of those arts' (Elder, 1978). This process of
selection needs to be examined in a way that does not necessarily
reduce the question to one of economics, as Elder is inclined to do.
Sponsorship needs to be considered in terms of money as well as
other practices. This is precisely the perspective that is available in
rethinking culture, which opens up the space to consider these
connections not as linear deterministic connections but as complex
articulations that incorporate a variety of other issues, particularly
religious practices in India.

One principal source of sponsorship were the religious centers
that provided the support for the production and maintenance of
particular artefacts, dance and musical forms that glorified particular
religious themes. This also resulted in the close connection between
religion and culture in India.

*Culture and Religion:* Religion also played a key role in artistic
production in India, where some of the 'best' works of classical
Indian art have been produced in temples and around the religious-
historic epics of Indian civilization. This is pointed out by Kinsley
in his book *Hinduism*: 'Indian culture is so saturated with Hinduism
(and other native Indian religions) that nearly all Indian art may
be considered religious in one way or the other' (Kinsley, 1982).
Kinsley elaborates on this in his discussion of specific expressions,
like the Hindu temples of Kandariya and the Kangra paintings of
Radha and Krishna. Similarly, other religious traditions, particularly Islam, influenced culture in India too. Elder points to the
Muslim Bahmani sultanates in the Deccan who financed impressive
architectural works.

The connection between religion and culture, particularly within
the tradition of high culture, again establishes a necessary relation

---

[7] Thus, Indian culture is conceptualized around a set of specific art forms (such
as Kangra paintings), or dance forms (such as Kathakali), or architecture (such as
the Ajanta and Ellora cave paintings). These are the ones that enjoyed sponsorship
and survived the tests of time. This is precisely why sponsorship is vital in thinking
about Indian culture.

between religious practices and cultural practices. High culture in India was indeed connected with religion, as the historical analysis of Kinsley points out. However, this connection does not preclude the possibility of other connections between cultural, religious and other practices.

## The Dominant Formulation of Culture in India

Within this history, culture remained a commodity that belonged to an elite group in society, who closely guarded this 'high' culture as authentic Indian culture. This included cultural expressions, such as classical dances like Kathakali and classical musical forms (Apte, 1978); ancient temple and cave sculptures and paintings, particularly those associated with Hinduism and its offshoots (Kinsley, 1982); and a variety of other traditional artistic expressions (including such mythological and religious epics as the Mahabharat and Ramayan). Culture was limited to a privileged set of artefacts and texts—those that were considered to be refined enough to be included within the preview of the elitist description of culture. There has always been a tendency in recounting Indian cultural history to relate culture with royalty and religion, (both of which represent two higher levels of social order) as well as the specific cultural expressions that enjoyed the patronage of royalty and religion.

Indian culture has also been conceptualized around specific stages in Indian history—representing the dominant royal order. There is, therefore, the ancient culture of the Aryans, followed by the culture related with Islamic insurgence, and then later the culture of the West represented by the British colonials, and more recently the high culture of the 'educated intellectual' of independent India. Instead of a critical perspective, however, a deterministic drive linked the moments with specific aesthetic expressions.[8]

Continuing this tendency to promote a theory of culture based on the purity of expression, culture has now been organized around specific bodies of aesthetic expression. The Sangeet Natak Akademi (Academy of Dance, Drama and Music) represents one of the best

[8] For instance, there are Mughal paintings, Hindu dances and Western music. These have been the markers of culture in India.

examples. Two other such academies were established in the early fifties to encourage the State sponsored development of specific arts. This was an attempt to restore the *greatness of the past*, particularly in restoring what were the monuments (both symbolic as well as material) of classical Indian high culture.

The key issues in understanding the mainstream theory of Indian culture, thus, lie in its historical heritage, elitist sponsorship, and its close relation with religion.[9] These are indeed the three criteria that are often used to test the authenticity and value of culture in India. The significance of this lies in the narrow interpretation of culture which marginalizes a variety of other practices that are also a significant part of the everyday life of the various social blocs in India. Culture in India needs to be considered in connection with the diversity of languages, religions and regions that India represents. It also needs to be considered in combination with the variety of practices around various cultural forms, such as cinema, television, theater, popular music and the folk manifestations of culture in rural theaters (such as 'yatra' and 'nautanki'). However, a historical framework that relies mainly on high culture in conceptualizing Indian culture often excludes the variety of other cultures that need to be examined in developing a theory of culture in India.

Moreover, a theory of culture that relies heavily on the high cultural tradition of India tends to separate culture and its relations with other practices into mutually exclusive relationships. As my early categorization indicates, the theory of culture in India tends to regard culture and tradition, culture and patronage, and culture and religion as separate connections which represent the complex nature of culture. These and other connections need to be explored in unity, finding the contradictions in these connections, and discovering the ideological nature of these connections.

There is thus a need to consider two key issues in rethinking Indian culture and moving the analysis away from a historical logic that recirculates a traditional notion of Indian culture. First, it is

---

[9] This is precisely what is still being debated, particularly in view of the growing connection between religion and a variety of other practices. As one critic, Sitaram Yechuri recently indicated: 'The greatest misdeed that is being done to the country today is that culture is being strait-jacketed with religion' (Yechuri, May 1991).

This is precisely the recirculation of the framework of cultural thinking that has dominated the Indian scenario for a long time.

important to recognize that there are a variety of cultures that are available in a cultural map of a country such as India. Thus, it is insufficient to think of one monolithic culture of India and a framework of culture needs to incorporate this variety. Secondly, it is important to be able to rethink culture as a unity of practices, within which a variety of practices—including the signifying practices of Doordarshan—can be included.

Both these notions are examined within the tradition of cultural studies, and this provides the point of departure for rethinking Indian culture, particularly within the framework of cultural studies, albeit as it developed in post-War Europe.

## The Plurality of Culture: Indian Culture(s)

In their influential pieces such as Hoggart's *The Uses of Literacy* (1957), some British scholars began to examine, through a historical perspective, the state of Britain in the tumultuous post-War period of reconstruction and resettlement. Their major break was in challenging the narrow notion of culture and rethinking culture not as a single 'culture' but a series of 'cultures'. This reconceptualization of culture is not specific to a particular region or history. It is possible to forward this argument about most regions of the world where a variety of traditions and practices coexist. Even though the histories are different, the work of scholars like Hall, offer a framework within which questions of region can be reframed to conceive of the culture(s) of the regions of India, recognizing the plural definition of culture(s). This multiple modality of culture is highlighted by Hall: 'Thompson insisted on the historical specificity of culture, on its plural, not singular definition—"cultures", not "Culture": above all, on the necessary struggle, contradiction and conflict between cultures' (Hall, 1980a)

This is precisely the theoretical position that needs to be adopted in rethinking culture in India. The concern for high classical Indian culture should not suggest that cultural practices in India are only limited to high culture. In contrast to high culture, there has always been a rich tapestry of other cultural practices that have permeated across the entire Indian system.

For instance, India is composed of a variety of regions, languages and religions, each with a unique set of cultural practices. These regions and languages represent regional cinema, television and literature in the local language, and are often connected with local religious dominance. Some of these practices have been excluded in the framework that considers the high culture of India as the authentic Indian culture. This leads to a marginalization of these other practices. In order to rethink culture in India, it is therefore crucial to find a way of incorporating these other practices within the framework of Indian culture. Every geographic region in India boasts of indigenous culture (for instance, folk culture in India is very region and language specific).[10] This makes it difficult to describe one Indian culture, and it is much more useful to think of the various culture(s) of India.

It is within this framework of cultures that one needs to place Doordarshan as yet another center around which a television culture is developing. This is indeed one of the many elements that produce the cultures of India. The strategy of Doordarshan lies in its use of signifying and representational practices that reproduce and recirculate, within the national arena, a variety of practices as the cultural practices of India. This also provides the point of departure to think of culture not only as a construct with multiple modalities, but also as a combination of a variety of practices.

This is the crucial link between Doordarshan and culture in India, just as it is the link between television and culture in any setting. It is important to recognize that cultures are the products of a combination of material practices. Among these material practices, the signifying practices of television are a crucial element.

[10] Elder writes about the variety of folk cultures in India. However, in his historical formulation, the differences between these traditions of folk culture are smoothed over. Yet it is important to recognize these differences, and rethink the question of culture as culture(s) in reading the following description provided by Elder:

The Tamil Vaishnavite 'alvars' and Shaivite 'nayanars' sang hymns of God's praise to the Tamil people in the villages through which they walked. Chaitanya's popularization of Bengali hymn singing, Surdas' and Mirabai's Hindi poems calling Krishna the divine conjugal lover, and Kabir's verses asserting the oneness of God were all directed to particular audiences sharing convictions about the nature of God and man's relationship to Him (Elder, 1978).

In this analysis, to find the similarities of theme, Elder loses sight of the intrinsic differences between language and the other practices that produce the distinct cultures of the Tamils, Bengalis and Hindi speakers.

Moreover, the practices of and around television are implicated by, and implicate, a variety of other practices that produce the cultures of a social group. It is therefore necessary to rethink the cultures of India as the combination of a variety of practices, and examine the modalities and the contradictory nature of everyday life material practices that produce the cultural space.

It is within this framework that it is also possible to make the distinction between a dominant culture and the cultures that, in combination, produce the cultural map of India. In thinking of cultures, there is an intrinsic rejection of any dominant culture as the authentic and preferred culture of a country or social bloc. Moreover, the notion of dominant culture as the 'true' and 'high' culture is also the preferred notion within the dominant theory of culture. This is precisely what is challenged within the perspective of cultural studies, which attempts to question the dominant culture, and rephrase culture not through its authenticity in artefacts, but in its system of practices within a structure of society.

## Culture as Practices

The previous section emphasized that it is myopic to think of one culture, particularly in a country such as India. It is much more generative to consider culture as a multi-dimensional entity with multiple tendencies made up of a variety of cultures. I shall now examine the nature of these cultures not only as artefacts but in terms of practices that, in combination, produce these various cultures.

The rethinking of culture as practices, and the reconsideration of cultural practices as distinct from other practices was examined within the structuralist moment of cultural studies. Structuralists shifted culture away from the premise of texts, value and ideals—in short, the entire 'humanities' definition of culture was examined. It became an investigation of the organization of human activity, the need to find the homologies between different activities, and the quest for an explanatory 'structure' that would shed light on the various manifestations of human activity. This was a way of examining the issue of culture, and introducing, into the equation, the basic tenet of structuralism: the question of form—the 'how' of culture and not the 'what'.[11] This examination was aimed particularly at the structures in society which attempted to reproduce culture as a set of practices that were preferred by the dominant social bloc. The question of 'what' was intimately connected with the question of 'how': it was important to investigate what particular practices were dominant within the constantly shifting hierarchy of society.

This break in cultural studies provides two significant generative notions. First, the rethinking of culture as practices and, secondly, the placement of these practices within a structured system, with its strategies of domination and subordination. This emphasizes that practices are not uniform, and in the production of culture, certain practices become preferred over others. It also identifies any textual locus of culture, emphasizing that it is important to examine the variety of practices that produce the various cultures. It was no longer possible to draw any necessary relationship between culture and artefact, but it was important to examine culture as a wider construct that incorporates a larger set of questions.

This insight helps to identify a framework of culture in India which is preoccupied with the temples, paintings and dances. It can now be argued that a theory of culture in India also needs to provide the space to include the practices of specific social blocs, and place all the related practices in relational positions within a structured hierarchy of society. There are now two interrelated issues: the notion of practices and the structured hierarchical relation between practices which, in turn, is connected with the dominance of particular social blocs at specific moments in history.

At various moments in history, the structure of Indian society witnessed different leadership, and at every such moment, the dominant bloc in the structure attempted to reproduce their practices as the preferred cultural practices of India. There are many examples which reflect the hierarchical structure of cultural practices—beginning from the dawn of Indian civilization, (when the invading Aryans subordinated the rich Dravidian culture) to the

[11] Just as Saussure was attempting to seek the *langue* as the organizing structure of language, and *parole* as the specific example of the structure, there was now a need to seek the organizations of culture to find the different ways in which particular cultural activities were made dominant, while others remained subordinate and marginalized in a well structured social order.

current media practice of giving Hindi precedence over other regional languages.[12]

Therefore, within this emerging conceptual framework of cultures, Doordarshan plays a dual role—first, the signifying practices produce the cultural form of Doordarshan, and then, within a structured social order, these practices are related to other practices that surround it. This generates two issues: the need to first examine the textual, narrative and generic practices of Doordarshan and then the other practices that surround the text, and the way Doordarshan is interrelated with a variety of other material everyday practices.

For instance, in India the viewing of a program like *Mahabharat* on television does not only constitute a reading practice, but is also a religious practice of worship, where the reader of television is participating in a religious activity by turning on the television set on a Sunday morning and involving the entire family in watching a 'religious soap opera'.[13] These constitute everyday activities which are related to the economic ability to own a television receiver, and the cultural/religious capital of already knowing the epic text, as well as the linguistic practice of speaking, or at least, understanding Hindi. These represent specific practices in which the reader participates. Meanwhile, the television text borrows and appropriates from a series of practices ranging from the signifying practices of cinema, and accepted religious practices that are recognizable by the reader of the text.

The consequence of conceptualizing culture as a set of practices, and examining the relation of practices, is to emphasize the nature of the relation between the practices, and to rethink the nature of practices themselves. It is here that the notion of culture as an articulation of practices becomes generative.

[12] Elder emphasizes this when describing the way in which the insurgence of Islam changed the cultural map of India, particularly when rulers such as Aurangzeb subordinated Hindu cultural practices, marginalizing them within a social structure where the Islamic rulers occupied the position of leadership.

[13] This is evident in the reaction that religious soap operas, particularly the *Ramayan*, obtained from the audience. There are reports that people, specially in the rural areas, considered the television set as an object of worship—particularly when the religious epics were broadcast.

## *Culture as an Articulation of Practices*

The notion of articulation is drawn from the works of Laclau. It was developed principally by Hall (1985, 1986a) as a theoretical principle about a non-reductionist and historical analysis of the relation between ideology, social forces and subjectivity. The term articulation in British usage has a dual meaning: on the one hand, it refers to utterances while, on the other hand, it refers to the way in which vehicles are chained together or 'articulated' together to form a whole, with the possibility of separation, without any necessary essentiality to the connections. In a similar way, Hall proposes that various elements in society are connected together in a non-necessary way forming provisional unities and creating temporary connections which, however, are produced as natural through a process of hegemonic struggle and domination.

The work of ideology[14] is to produce these articulations as natural. At specific historic moments, unique connections are forged between different elements. However, the theory of articulation identifies this mystifying tendency by emphasizing the non-necessary nature of the connections, the lack of determinacy in the connections, the lack of anything absolute about the connections and the non-essential nature of the connections. This was a way to move away from the deterministic notion of necessary relationships between class position, ideology, material practices, culture and experience. Here the focus is on the notion that there are no necessary connections between these elements but, in fact, these are unities that are artificially produced and are open to question and challenge.[15]

---

[14] The notion of ideology and ideological struggle will be elaborated in the next section.

[15] In the words of Hall:

the theory of articulation as I use it has been developed by Eernest Laclau, in his book *Politics and Ideology in Marxist Theory*. His argument there is that the political connotation of ideological elements have no necessary belongingness, and thus, we need to think the contingent, non-necessary, connection between different practices—between ideology and social forces, and between different elements within ideology, and between different social groups composing a social movement, etc. He uses the notion of articulation to break the necessatarian and reductionist logic which has dogged the classical marxist theory of ideology (Hall, 1986a).

In rethinking culture in India, the theory of articulation becomes particularly useful. Most of the connections encountered in Indian culture are indeed non-essential and can be (and need to be) thrown open for questioning. For example, when considering the relationship between religion and culture in India, this is the kind of combination that is encountered. In claiming that high culture in India is closely connected with religion, it is assumed that the connection is natural and preferred. Consequently, the connection becomes naturalized and dominant. Furthermore, the articulation between Hinduism and high culture becomes dominant where the cultural practices that are connected with other religions are marginalized. Similarly, in appropriating the Hindu practices depicted in *Mahabharat*, and reproducing and recirculating them, Doordarshan is able to emphasize the authenticity of Hindu practices as the central cultural practices of India. This is the articulation that is produced as natural and dominant, mystifying the non-essential nature of the articulations.

The fact that articulations are non-essential, and are a product of hegemonic struggles working through ideology, opens up the possibility of arguing for the field of ideological struggle through which such articulations are broken and rearticulated in new and different ways, opening up the space to accommodate the voice of the subordinate. [16] Hall has labelled this process ideological struggle because, in the end, the work of ideology is to forge chains of equivalence, and it is through a process of ideological struggle that these chains are broken and reformed. In Hall's words:

> a particular ideological chain becomes a site of struggle, not only when people try to displace, rupture or contest it by supplanting it with some wholly new alternative set of terms,

---

I have used this rather lengthy quote from Hall because it becomes the kernel of numerous future work by Hall and others to delve into the intricacies of several different social phenomenon, movements and practices, and has proved to be quite productive in its epistemological value.

[16] This is precisely the endeavor that people such as Gilroy and others are engaged in. Their key attempt has been to point out the non-essential nature of the connections and pose them as a problematic that is open for rethinking and rearticulation. Working on the question of race in Britain, Gilroy and others have questioned the naturalizing tendency that articulated race with economics. In their formulation, this is a non-essential connection that needs to be examined within the theory of articulation.

but also when they interrupt the ideological field and try to transform its meaning by changing or rearticulating its associations, for example, from the negative to the positive (Hall, 1985).

This can be illustrated by taking the name 'Ram' and seeing how its connotation and meaning has shifted over time, through a series of struggles, from one connected with wisdom, truthfulness and courage to the more recent connection with his birthplace and Hindu fanaticism.[17] In a similar way, most hegemonically produced articulations are open to struggle and it is possible to break apart the chains of equivalence to produce a new set of articulations that represent a different set of unities forged through struggle.

The dominant theory of culture in India ignores the possibility that the articulations that produce culture are also open to question and rethinking. Yet the material changes in the cultural arena are representative of this precise process where past articulations that produced culture and meaning are being broken and replaced by new articulations. For instance, the typical folk theater of West Bengal has always been connected with a folk interpretation of mythology.[18] When the grassroot leftist movement in the region began to dearticulate this connection and rearticulate the theatrical expression with narratives of oppression of the landless peasants, the entire popular culture around these dramatic formations changed, just as the effectivity of these dramatic formations was redefined (Bharucha, 1983). Yet a perspective of articulation is not a possibility which Bharucha explores in his book on these theaters of revolution.

[17] Ram is the protagonist in the epic *Ramayan*. Recently, there have been violent debates about the location of his birthplace in northern India. It has been argued that the Muslim invaders of the past have desecrated the exact spot of Ram's birthplace by constructing a mosque there. Hindu fundamentalists have now demolished the mosque and are trying to construct a temple there. This has been a center around which there has been an upsurge of Hindu fanaticism and militicism, leading to subsequent bloody Hindu-Muslim riots.

[18] The popular folk theater, also called the *yatra*, can be considered the commonest popular cultural formation of rural West Bengal. The practice of attending the *yatra* is connected with several other practices, like going to the carnival surrounding the *yatra*. All these practices articulate together into one specific popular cultural formation. The closest analogy to the *yatra* is perhaps the American vaudeville shows.

The framework to conceptualize culture incorporates a number of elements. First, in a country such as India, culture needs to be moved away from a monolithic concept of high culture. A variety of other cultures need to be considered in rethinking culture in India. Secondly, these cultures need to be considered as practices, where cultural practices are a part of the variety of practices that are placed within a structured society. Finally, these practices are often articulated together in nonessential ways where certain connections are produced as desirable and natural. This also opens up the space for struggle where practices can be dearticulated to produce new articulations that would produce different cultures.

Consequently, two issues now merit further attention. First, the notion of practices needs to be examined to discover their various conflictual relations and, secondly, the contradictions between practices need to be examined in terms of an ideological struggle.

## *Culture, Multidimensional Practices and Ideology*

Having established that culture is made up of practices, it is indeed easy to accept that there are only a limited set of activities that are the natural practices for a social group, and attempt to describe such a limited and harmonious set of practices as the 'cultural' practices of the social group. For instance, this tendency is exposed in Geertz's (1973) work on the different south Asian nations. The primary aim and outcome of this work is the identification of a limited set of practices which are supposed to be the best indicators of the culture of specific groups of people.

Theoretical approaches, like that of Geertz, assume that practices are harmonious sets of symbolic, cultural, social and economic activities that are natural, necessary and unique for specific communities of people. And when culture is theorized as a set of harmonious practices, culture itself tends to become monolithic and centralized. It is precisely here that the mystifying notion of a centralized and common culture becomes embedded and naturalized. It is, therefore, important to recognize that practices are multidimensional, and often contradictory, and are in conflict with each other. This is acknowledged when exploring the relation between culture, ideology and ideological struggle, and examining the connections between practices, ideology and ideological struggle, where various practices struggle with each other to gain a position of dominance.

However, in thinking of Indian culture, this particular struggle has not been the focus of attention. For instance Bharucha (1983), in his book on village drama in West Bengal and its transformation into vehicles of political signification, only draws a historical analysis of the development of the alternative, not necessarily locating it within any particular set of ideological struggles.[19]

The tendency to smooth over the contradictions and the multi-dimensionality of practices is also evident when thinking about Doordarshan. In considering the practices around television and the signifying practices of Doordarshan, there is also a tendency to naturalize the practices of Doordarshan, and accept them unequivocally. Thus, the signifying practices that are in opposition to the hegemony of the Hindu-Hindi bloc are either marginalized or brought back into the mainstream, mystifying their conflictual relation with the leadership. However, given the articulated nature of practices, the signifying practices of television are also engaged in an ideological struggle to reproduce certain practices as dominant and natural. This is precisely why it is important to recognize the ideological nature of these signifying practices. As a corollary, by examining the signifying practices of television it is possible to unearth the ideological practices that implicate the practices of television. It is important to establish the connection between cultural practices (such as the signifying practices of Doordarshan) and ideology to examine the multidimensional relationship between the two.

This connection can be traced in the relationship between cultural domination and ideological struggle. The ruling bloc has constantly been able to occupy a position of cultural domination primarily by its ability to control what is broadcast on Doordarshan. These broadcast decisions have been taken by the social bloc who have been able to occupy the position of leadership in Delhi. It has been

---

[19] Where struggle has been discussed, the tendency has been towards a reductionist argument, falling back within the base/superstructure metaphor, reducing questions to their last economic instance.

the cultural practices of these social blocs that have been circulated on television. However, in the earlier stages of Doordarshan, particularly before the broadcast of such powerful programs such as *Mahabharat* and *Ramayan*, the struggle was over a set of cultural practices around language and ethnic practices. Here, the question of ideology is combined with the questions of culture through hegemonic struggle, where the social group that occupies the position of leadership is able to combine its preferred cultural practices with a series of other practices of everyday life. This is not only the relationship between the notion of cultural domination and ideological struggle for hegemony, but also the moment when the two become related and thus are able to work in unison to strengthen the consensual position of leadership of a particular social bloc.

However, the notion of hegemony, as discussed by Gramsci and later by Hall, also provides the space for a series of struggles, where the war of attrition is not only over the primacy of one set of cultural practices over others, but also with respect to a set of other practices (such as religious, economic and political practices). In combining the questions of religion and politics in India, the struggle for hegemony is waged on many fronts, among which the cultural site of television plays a significant role.

In the realm of culture, there is a struggle over a set of practices that will be produced as the dominant ones, marginalizing others as subordinate, marginal or counter-cultural. Within India, particular social blocs are able to carve a position of leadership, and thus circulate their practices as the preferred and dominant ones. This question of leadership becomes crucial in this formulation, since the leading social bloc enjoys the position from which they can reshape the entire cultural map of a country. In terms of Doordarshan and Indian culture, this is crucial since the medium is owned by the government, and the cultural practices that Doordarshan reproduces and circulates often reflects the practices and the ideology of the leading social bloc.

The question of leadership is examined by Gramsci (See Gramsci, 1971; Forgcas, 1988) who elaborates on the question of leadership and struggle in formulating the notion of 'hegemony' and hegemonic struggle. Gramsci rejects any need to align cultural, ideological and economic questions in any causal chain. Instead, he speaks of a historical alliance of social formations into social blocs, which enjoy dominant status by establishing a position of leadership for the subordinate social blocs. This is the essence of the hegemonic struggle—the battle to maintain a position of leadership, and thus have the ability to naturalize a set of cultural and social practices as natural at a particular moment in history. This represents the way in which a specific set of cultural practices, under the stewardship of the leaders (in Gramsci's writing, these are the intellectuals), become the dominant ones. However, this is not guaranteed and, given the non-necessary nature of these relationships, they are open to challenge and disruption.

This is precisely the project of television planners in India—to wage a hegemonic struggle and forge a particular image of the nation and national culture on television. This is done by appropriating from the mainstream as well as the marginal, and forging a provisional, but ideologically naturalized unity and circulating and recirculating that as the dominant and preferred one. The effectivity of this enterprise is partly exposed in the increasing search for a central religious tenet, perhaps manifested in increasing Hindu fundamentalism and its successful quest for a material center in the birthplace of Ram, the traditional Hindu demagogue, recently reproduced in the serial *Ramayan*.[20] The struggle is over a set of practices—signifying practices—around television, where the aim is to produce one particular signifying practice—the 'religious soap opera'—as the dominant national cultural signifying practice. This, in turn, is articulated with the religious practices of Hinduism—the religion of the leading social bloc in India now. However, since these connections are not guaranteed, a close textual analysis can demystify the processes that forge these unities, and open up the articulations to questioning.

Summarizing briefly, it is possible to argue that the traditional framework conceptualizing culture in India was preoccupied with a formulation that was classical-elitist. Within this, the three key tendencies were to think of culture in terms of its historical authenticity, its ability to attract elite sponsorship, and its close connection with religion—particularly Hinduism.

[20] The important point to note here is that Hinduism had never had or needed such a center. Traditionally, Hinduism represents a philosophy, a way of life, not a religious faith that is necessarily centered around one place or person. Hinduism never had a Christ or Mohammed, but was manifest in many different beliefs about a way of life.

In a reworked framework of culture in India, it is possible to recognize the variety of cultures in India organized around diverse contradictory factors. Furthermore, it is important to acknowledge the material nature of culture, in its manifestation in everyday practices. These practices are sometimes contradictory, and they are connected together in chains of equivalence, and articulated together in non-essential ways. Consequently, there is a possibility of waging an ideological struggle to break these chains, and identify the relations between the practices. Ideology works to naturalize these chains and perpetuate the hegemony of specific dominant social blocs at any moment in time. This complex reworking therefore, frees culture from the reductionist notion which reduces it to an artefact and relates culture with unidimensional vectors,[21] such as religion or economic class. Indeed, this theory of culture emphasizes the material, ideological and relational nature of culture.

As a final example I will cite Bengali culture, which I feel most familiar with. This is not a culture that is only connected with the reading of Bengali literature, but is also connected with a Bengali way of life, including the variety of practices, such as food habits, social relations, religious practices, and the signifying and reading practices around Doordarshan, both in its regional broadcasts from Calcutta as well as the Delhi based National Network. At the same time, these are not guaranteed connections, and are open to question and challenge. It is within such a dynamic notion of culture that one needs to place the question of Doordarshan, and examine the ways in which it is connected with a variety of other practices.

## Indian Culture and Doordarshan

By using the argument that culture is made up of a set of practices, it is possible to claim that culture is, in fact, an ideological construct made up of a set of material practices that have been established as dominant, natural and normal through the workings of an ideological struggle, provisionally reflecting the hegemony of a social bloc.

---

[21] Used again in terms of a social force with a direction and magnitude.

Further, it can be argued that the texts of Doordarshan circulate a set of practices by reproducing them on television. These are produced as the dominant and preferred practices, marginalizing other practices that have not been able to win the struggle for representation. This is precisely how the television text begins to play a role in the production of the popular culture of India. For example, the reproduction of the always-already text of *Mahabharat* only emphasizes the centrality of Hindu practices in describing the cultural space of India. One fundamental purpose of this study is to reexamine the text and demystify the processes by which particular practices and ideologies become naturalized.

Doordarshan relates to different practices at a variety of levels. At one level, Doordarshan is textually connected with other signifying practices within the cultural space. Television in India does not work in a cultural vacuum, particularly when culture is reconceptualized as the combination of a variety of practices. Doordarshan is ultimately connected to the other cultural and social practices, and the production of meaning from the television text is overdetermined and multiply determined by its connections with other cultural, social and signifying practices.

Secondly, given the non-necessary articulation of the practices that produce Indian culture and cultural space, it is possible to break the connections and forge new connections that ultimately redefine cultural space. Within this dynamic picture of culture, the position of Doordarshan in the cultural map is not static but constantly shifts with the way in which television appropriates other practices within its own signifying practices.

In a culture that is a product of the articulation of practices, the position and role of Doordarshan can be better understood by examining the various signifying practices used by television. These practices help to describe what is being circulated at any moment as preferred and dominant. For example, the narrative and generic practices of Doordarshan have been reproducing a Hindi-centered set of practices. This has slowly been naturalized, and it is increasingly accepted that the National Network is a predominantly Hindi transmission.

Thus, within this framework of conceptualizing Indian culture, and the recognition that the signifying practices of television are an integral element in this cultural space, it is possible to argue that greater emphasis needs to be placed on the rethinking of Doordarshan as a cultural practice. The significant manifestation of Doordarshan is in textual, narrative and generic practices. This suggests the need to examine the various textual strategies of television, now providing the point of departure for an overview of textual analysis— the focus of the next chapter.

# 3

# Doordarshan: A Critical Glance[1]

*Crucial assumptions and propositions, not simply
in ideology or in conscious stance, but in the ebb
and flow of feelings from and to others, in assumed
situations and relationships, and in the relationships
implied or proposed within the immediate uses of
language, are always present and always directly
significant. In many instances, and especially in
class-divided societies, it is necessary to make them
explicit, by analysis, and to show, in detail, that
this is not a case of going 'beyond' the literary
work, but of going more thoroughly into its full
expressive significance.*

**Raymond Williams**, *Marxism and Literature*

**A critical reconsideration** of culture as the articulation of a variety
of practices not only widens and enriches the conceptualization of
culture, but also calls for a critical examination of the various
articulated elements. Any element in the chain that makes up
culture needs to be understood both in terms of its structural
position in the chain as well as the unique element that it is.
Consequently, to understand the role that television plays in the

[1] Television formation refers to the duality of television where it is a cultural
aesthetic form by itself while it also produces or 'forms' popular culture around the
television texts and narratives.

Indian cultural arena, it is important to reexamine television formation as an independent cultural element. One possible way to
conduct this critical examination is by considering the variety of
texts that are available on television, ferreting out the ways in
which texts demonstrate similar and opposing representational
tendencies, finally focusing on one set of similar texts to examine
them in depth to obtain some conclusions about the position of
Doordarshan in Indian culture. In this selective examination of
Doordarshan, my concern is with two primary kinds of texts on
television: educational and entertainment.

Over the past three decades, a variety of texts have evolved on
Doordarshan. At present, Doordarshan offers a wide range of
texts to its audience. However, this variety is not unlimited and it
is possible to identify similar and opposing textual and signifying
practices on Doordarshan that can be used to classify the variety of
texts into ordered groups. These groups not only represent the
limits and boundaries of textual practices but also the process by
which these tendencies develop. This is the realm of genre analysis
where the focus is on two aspects of representational practices:
first, on the question of order and classification and, secondly, on
the question of process—the way in which genres develop and are
legitimized.[2] I would argue that, in the case of Doordarshan, the
classification of genres follows a specific set of steps—a process by
which genres developed in India.

The significance of genre analysis is in both these aspects of
genre. Genres not only assist in understanding how the texts on
television are related to each other, but also elaborate the ways in
which these relationships develop and evolve. The position of any
text within a genre is implicated by its internal characteristics as
well as the relations of the text with other texts that surround it.

In the case of Doordarshan, the development of genres has been
influenced by four interrelated factors. First, due to the relative
infancy of television in India, Doordarshan was able to borrow
many of the representational strategies that signify various genres

---

[2] The notion of genre as a process is elaborated by Neale (1990) where he
identifies three aspects of the process in his essay 'Questions of Genre.' The three
levels of rethinking genre as a process involves the following: 'the level of expectation,
the level of the generic corpus, and the level of "rules" and "norms" that govern
both' (Neale, 1990). All these 'levels,' as Neale puts it, are operative in the
development of genres in India.

from countries with a larger history of television. Secondly, the vocabulary of genres (for example, labels such as 'news' and 'soap operas') were appropriated from the existing lexicon of popular cultures where television was a well established cultural formation. Third, this vocabulary was quickly naturalized and circulated by the secondary and tertiary texts that surround television. Finally, television producers in India were quick to appropriate the various signifying strategies that distinguish between these already available labels. These factors are well illustrated in the way educational programs developed on Indian television.

When television was instituted in India, a large amount of research was focused on what the nature of programs ought to be on Doordarshan. In order to arrive at a decision, the first Chanda Commission took a close look at the functioning of the Italian television system. This led them to identify a class of programs that were instructional in nature. The programs offered a model for the development of textual strategies for similar programs on Doordarshan. This represents the first tendency in genre development in India, where the textual characteristics of a particular type of West European television broadcast was adapted for Indian television, albeit after considerable recoding for Indian culture.[3]

The second tendency of genre development is illustrated in the adoption of the label 'educational programs'. This term was already in use in Western Europe, and it was quickly appropriated by the Indian television industry to signify the class of instructional programs. A set of programs developed that were labelled 'educational programs' and were recognized as an integral part of Doordarshan. This tendency also represents the development of genres through institutional discourse. Labels such as 'educational programs', 'news' and 'sports' represent a set of institutional standards for Doordarshan. This is what Ellis (1981) refers to in talking about films: 'An idea of the film is widely circulated and promoted, an idea which can be called the "narrative image" of the film, the cinema's anticipatory reply to the question, "What is the film like?"' (Ellis, 1981). This is precisely the process that occurs in the case of genre development on Doordarshan where the industry is able to circulate, across a secondary text, a clear anticipatory

---

[3] This is also encountered in the development of soap operas in India, when there was a period of close collaboration between Televisa of Mexico and Doordarshan.

image of the program to be broadcast. Moreover, secondary texts, such as the popular press, quickly adapted the same labels in describing the programs in their reviews, television program listing and in the common parlance of television.

Very quickly, a set of expectations developed where the audience would expect a set of educational programs at specific time slots. Further, the audience would anticipate a repetitive set of textual strategies that would be used in educational programs. This is the question of verisimilitude.[4] Educational programs have been able to develop a system of expectations in the audience, where the reader can anticipate a particular set of norms and laws in the instructional programs. Similarly, a set of expectations have developed concerning news, sports and childrens'programs, for instance. This notion of expectation and verisimilitude also represents the fourth way in which genres have developed in India: television producers have been able to construct a set of conventions that are now recognized, expected and found probable for particular genres of programs by the viewing audience.[5]

Summarizing briefly, the notion of genre on Doordarshan has now been well codified and the various texts on Doordarshan can be classified into specific genres based on a variety of aspects that include the establishment of industry standards and the combination of specific sets of representational strategies that have finally led to the audience expecting a set of conventions for specific genres. These genres include a large range of programs that can be examined around a set of binary relationships that constitute the chief contradictions on Doordarshan as well as in Indian popular culture.[6]

One such polar relationship is between entertainment and education, I have chosen to use this as the primary opposition since my final aim is to examine a particular entertainment program as the focus of analysis. The programs on Doordarshan have always

[4] The notion of verisimilitude involves issues of similarity, plausibility and expectation. Neale (1990) expands on the question of verisimilitude, arguing that genres are composed of a set of expectations based on what is probable within a particular generic corpus.

[5] This is also what Feuer would call the ritualistic and ideological aspects of genre where the audience comes to assume a set of signifying characteristics as 'natural' for a particular genre.

[6] A variety of binary relations can be used in such an analysis. These include the relations between rural:urban, Hindi:non-Hindi, education:entertainment, and so on.

been classified, both by the industry and its affiliates, as well as the audience, into these two broad categories. As I have indicated in the first chapter, the notion of education on television is determined by a belief that programs that instruct the audience about a particular issue can be considered educational. Consequently, the logic of the development of the genre of the educational program is intimately connected with the rationale for the introduction of television technology in India—primarily as a medium that would be able to solve the problem of setting up schools in remote areas. Television was conceived as a 'tool' that would become the center around which an entire instructional institution would develop. Luthra (1986) points out that the initial set of programs that were broadcast from New Delhi between 1965 and 1973 were primarily aimed at school children and farmers who did not have access to a school infrastructure but depended on television as a primary source of instruction.[7]

From this origin, the corpus of programs that have evolved as the educational broadcasts of Doordarshan are signified by a set of factors that determine the limits and scope of the text of these programs. These are programs that use similar signifying strategies to impart factual information to the audience. Consequently, the audience recognizes these programs as ones that have specific purpose and style. Yet, these programs are not composed of a restrictive set of signifying practices but, within the broad limitations of instruction, a variety of textual strategies have developed.

The more common form of educational program is a classroom-like format where one or more experts discuss issues such as farming, agriculture, hygiene and family planning. In the earlier stages of television in India, this was perhaps the commonest form of educational broadcast, and included programs such as *Krishi Darshan* (a program for farmers) and *Pallikatha* (a program meant for the rural, or *palli*, sector of India). However, the stylistic limits of the didactic presentation were tested both by the producers as well as the audience. With the increasing presence of non-educational programs, particularly feature films and feature film based

---

[7] This also led to the interest in 'Teleclubs' as centers where a group of people could watch a community television, in a semi-classroom setting, further increasing the significance of television as an educational tool, and strengthening the importance of 'educational' programs on television (Luthra, 1986).

programs, the producers began to realize that educational broadcasts were losing popularity as the audience began to expect something beyond dry instructional fare. This led to a broadening of the
scope and style of educational programs.

Increasingly, the programs began to use textual strategies like
quiz and game shows, dramatization and talk shows. Among these
strategies, the talk show has now become a standard and well
recognized strategy on Doordarshan. Talk shows comprise of a set
of experts, and a host who will facilitate a discussion on a particular
issue which could be of importance to the viewers. Talk shows
have further diversified into shows for children, youth and women.
Youth programs aim at questions that are pertinent to the emerging
youth culture of India while women's programs attempt to identify
the various challenges that women face in India today. Children's
programs, on the other hand, deal with issues that will be of
interest to youngsters, always maintaining a balance between attractive presentation and instruction. This stylistic balance is a key
factor in examining educational programs in India today.

The increasing presence of a variety of entertainment programs,
ranging from the feature film to the serialized soap opera, has
challenged the educational programs. The genre has transformed
to appropriate from other signifying practices in order to make the
instructional programs attractive to the audience. This process has
stretched the limits of the educational text, constantly bringing it
closer to what would more often be called entertainment. In some
ways the distinction between education and entertainment has
become increasingly fuzzy, as educational programs have appropriated not only from the entertainment styles of Doordarshan,
but have also relied on imported fare. A large number of the
afternoon educational broadcasts use material from BBC, CBC and
the American Information Services. Furthermore, the University
Grants Commission (UGC) of the Indian government has sponsored
the development of indigenous instructional programs that move
away from the 'talking head' style to a more elaborate text that
uses visually attractive graphics, expert presenters and outdoor
footage.

In summary, the corpus of educational programs is now a diffused
set of texts. The audience has learned to expect a certain amount
of instructional material presented in a signifying style that is
closer to the style of soap operas and feature films than the

classroom lecture format. This suggests that the genre of educational programs has come closer to merging with the entertainment programs, and it has become increasingly difficult to draw a distinction between the two.

One manner in which the distinction is still made is in the way secondary texts describe the programs, and the expectation of the audience regarding a particular program. For example, in the July 1991 television program guide section of a Calcutta daily, *The Telegraph*, programs were described as the 'UGC Countrywide Classroom', which included sub-headings such as 'Simplification of Switching Circuits II; Mental Illness—A Diagnosis; Solar Passive House II.' This is precisely how the programs are placed within specific classes, and the audience expects to view instructional fare. Moreover, the overlap between education and entertainment programs, and the ambiguity of classification, is characterized in a title like 'Program on Environment'. In this instance, categorization becomes dubious and, from both textual and contextual concerns, the programs lie between entertainment and education.[8]

One group of programs that can be placed between entertainment and education are sports programs. Sports programs are often represented both as educational and entertainment. In its educational aspects, sports programs instruct the audience about a variety of sports, both national and international. At the same time, sports programs remain entertaining events to watch on television.

The corpus of programs that I have called entertainment programs includes a large variety primarily based on three characteristics. First, they do not make any pretence of imparting instruction; secondly, they are distinguished from educational broadcasts by the producer, the audience as well all the texts that surround Doordarshan; and, finally, they are bound within a set of textual limits that frame this class of programs.

Within the evolution of programs on Doordarshan, entertainment programs were closely aligned with two popular cultural elements—theater and the feature film. Entertainment programs

---

[8] Intimately connected to this argument is the issue of 'agency' in genre development. It is increasingly difficult to locate the origin of genres and who produces them. It is indeed a combination of industry standards, secondary texts and the audience that becomes the motive force behind the emergence and transformation of genres.

on Doordarshan appropriated liberally from these cultural formations, eventually developing a set of texts that were unique to
Doordarshan. This process of appropriation and recoding is illustrated in the body of programs that can be categorized as tele-plays
or plays broadcast on television.

In its initial manifestations, the television play remained a broadcast of the stage theater without the use of any specific televisual
styles. In these instances, the play would be performed on stage
and would simply be telecast as a stage production. However, as
techniques matured, the notions of visual space and light were
reexamined and the plays were transformed into 'tele-plays', where
multiple cameras, shot/reverse shot, eye-line matching and a variety
of other textual strategies were used to develop the tele-play as a
well defined set of programs.

In their present form, tele-plays are often based on the works of
well known authors which are recoded for the television screen.
However, they bring with them the baggage of the original author's
text, and provide the audience an anchor by which to make sense
of the program. For instance, in West Bengal, a tele-play based on
the work of Rabindranath Tagore, the Nobel Prize winning Bengali
poet, would provide the audience the necessary context within
which to place the television program. Moreover, these programs
are also inter-textual with the tradition of radio plays, which is an
important element in the radio program format of All India Radio
and its regional stations.

The significance of tele-plays lies in the fact that these programs
began to establish the necessary relationship between the audience
and the producer, principally by reminding the audience that
television offers a different body of entertainment from cinema,
radio and the stage. Tele-plays could bring actors and actresses
and the narrative much closer to the audience as compared to the
stage. At the same time, tele-plays were not necessarily self-
contained like film texts; indeed, tele-plays were a part of the
larger array of programs that made up the set of television programs on any evening. Finally, tele-plays provided a sense of
continuity, where a tele-play is expected every week, and this is
the fundamental characteristic of serial programs on television.

Tele-plays, thus, set the stage for the development of television
serials, which would effectively use the tele-play format, prolong
the narrative over a long period, and make the production closer

.to the feature film tradition. It is, therefore, not by accident that serialized programs were later in arriving than tele-plays and feature films on television. These earlier programs set the stage for the arrival of serialized programs. Feature film based programs, and the regular screening of feature films, also facilitated this process, primarily by establishing entertainment programs as a principal element of Doordarshan.

The introduction of feature films based programs was also intimately tied to the development of television technology in India. At a time when television was still establishing itself as a technological possibility in India, there was a need to supplement educational broadcasts with other programs that would provide a lighter mood for the television viewers (Luthra, 1986). The easiest and cheapest answer was found in the use of feature films for telecast on weekends. This was supplemented by the adoption of feature films based music for television. In both these endeavors, the underlying assumption was that feature films were a key and popular element in Indian culture and the use of feature film on television would be a guaranteed way of providing entertainment programs on Doordarshan.

Among the feature film based programs, perhaps the most popular and attractive were the ones that used musical segments from various films and put them together in a half hour potpourri of film music programs, such as *Chitrahaar* and *Chitramala* (both meaning a garland of films). These programs established the inter-textual relation between television and film, placing television in an inter-textual relation with film within the popular culture of India.

It is important to recognize that feature films and feature film based music are perhaps the two most important aspects of Indian popular culture. With the prolific production of Hindi films, each with a staple of half a dozen song and dance sequences, there was never a dearth of popular music in the cultural arena. For instance, All India Radio had regular request lines for film based music. Indeed, feature film based music is rated in a way similar to the American 'Top 40'. For example, the series of Sunday afternoon programs sponsored by the Binaca toothpaste company have continued to flourish on the commercial channel of All India Radio. In these programs, the top rated film songs of the week are played. The issue here is that film music is a key element in Indian popular culture and the feature film based music programs on Doordarshan offer an important inter-textual link between Doordarshan and feature films in India.

While songs and musical scores are available on record and on radio, Doordarshan was able to bring to the audience an additional aspect of feature film based music that radio and records could not—the visual image of the dance that accompanied the song and the actors and actresses who performed the dances. As Kobita Sarkar (1975) has pointed out, feature film based music is always performed by a small number of playback singers, and the actors and actresses lipsycnh with the songs. While the playback voice was available on radio and records, the holistic experience of listening to the music and watching the gyrations of a favorite actors or actresses, was only provided by Doordarshan. Compared to the feature film based music programs, the other song and dance programs appear distinctly lifeless since the Doordarshan studios cannot replicate the elaborate sets of India's Hollywood at Bombay.

Feature films, and feature film based programs, are therefore significant in two ways. First, these programs establish the relationship between films and television in Indian popular culture. No other corpus of programs did as much to popularize television as feature films and film music programs.[9] This inter-textuality would also provide the foundation for the second significance of these programs—the emergence of a body of programs that would appropriate from the textual strategies of feature films, and the tele-plays, to develop an entire new body of text that has loosely been called 'soap operas'.

The feature film industry, along with the experience gained in the production of tele-plays, provided the guidelines for the development of the soap opera text. This happened in a variety of ways (Mitra, 1988a). First, there was a transfer of talent from the feature film industry into the Doordarshan industry. Producers, actors and directors flocked to produce programs for Doordarshan, particularly after the introduction of color and the liberalization of

[9] In 1988, when Doordarshan suddenly decided to discontinue the *Chitramala* program in Calcutta, an article in a newspaper reported that the program had a '50 per cent viewership,' and ranked third in popularity among Calcutta Doordarshan programs (*The Telegraph*, June 1988). This only underscores the popularity of the feature film based programs.

the commercial advertising policies of Doordarshan. Secondly, these people brought with them the semiotic baggage of the Indian film text, quickly appropriating the Indian film style, with its liberal use of music, song, dance, violent fights and melodrama into the television soap opera.[10] However, there was a complex process of recoding, where the soap operas retained some of the aspects of cinematic style, the style developed for tele-plays, and adapted from the soap opera style of the countries with a longer history of soap operas. Thus the emergent soaps on Indian television were an interesting mixture of a variety of influences that produced a unique textual form on Doordarshan. Consequently, it is useful to deliberate on the use and meaning of the label 'soap opera' in the case of Doordarshan.

Within the context of Doordarshan, the terms 'soap opera' and 'serialized programs' are often used interchangeably. This is of primary importance, since the way in which these two names entered the Doordarshan vocabulary signify the relation between the terms and the corpus of texts they refer to. The label 'soap opera' was appropriated from the Western lexicon of television terms. The secondary texts surrounding Doordarshan are the primary users of this term. For instance, when the *Ramayan* text was adapted for television, a leading national weekly (*Sunday*) quickly labelled it as the 'Soap Opera of the Gods'—establishing its intertextuality with the genre of 'soap operas' as well as underscoring its religious connotation.

Academic research on Doordarshan also uses the label 'soap opera' in a relatively loose sense. For instance, Singhal and Rogers (1987) propose that some soap operas in India are 'pro-development'. In their definition, a pro-development soap opera is one that has the dual purpose of entertainment and education. They also argue that such soap operas are popular in Third World countries, placing the origin of these soap operas in the productions of Miguel Sabido of Televis, the Mexican commercial network. This is significant since one of the earlier soap operas on Doordarshan was conceived in a joint meeting with the Mexican counterparts of the Indian Ministry of Information and Broadcasting. What is important here is that the term 'soap opera' has been

---

[10] For a deeper analysis of the Indian Hindi film, it is useful to turn to authors such as Chidananda Das Gupta (1980, 1981) and Kobita Sarkar (1975) who lay out insightful descriptions of the Indian film.

appropriated from outside to describe a corpus of programs on Doordarshan that has little to do with the cultures from which the label has been appropriated. It is more a matter of convenience, I argue, that leads to this process, where the term soap opera offers a recognizable term to describe a diverse body of programs on Doordarshan. It is precisely for this reason that in India it is important to attach an additional qualifier such as 'pro-development', 'religious' or 'social' to further classify these programs. Also, it is for this reason that it is useful to approach these programs from a generic consideration that concentrates not on labeling by using preexisting lists, but on textual limitations and characteristics that set these programs aside from the other fare on television.[11]

The primary distinguishing characteristic of the body of programs that have loosely been called soap operas is their sense of continuity. These programs are serialized programs that are composed of a large number of episodes, each with their internal closure, but with a continuity that motivates the audience to watch the following episode. In this respect, these programs are structurally similar to the soap operas of the West.[12] Allen points out that soap operas in the United States have a paradigmatic structure consisting of a large number of characters and a syntagmatic structure where the narrative never ends but a major narrative question is left unanswered at the end of each episode. This is precisely what serialized programs achieve in India, be it 'pro-development' programs like *Humlog* or the ones about the Gods, such as *Ramayan* and *Mahabharat*. Finally, the TV guide in newspapers recognize this characteristic when describing these programs as serialized programs and not necessarily as soap operas.

Within this structurally similar corpus of serialized programs, there are a number of differences which provide the reason, and

[11] This is precisely what Allen (1983, 1985) posits about soap operas, where he argues that soap operas, on American television, follow a set of codes, and textual conventions that distinguish them from other texts, and include them in the corpus that has been called soap operas. The argument here is for finding structural conditions in the text that limit the text and place it in similar categories.

[12] This is precisely where I disagree with the Singhal and Rogers assertion that 'pro-development television soap operas in Third World nations are quite different from television soap operas in the United States.' Structurally, there are many similarities, and it is these similarities that provide the legitimacy for the term 'soap opera'.

the need, to categorize them as social, religious, pro-development, and so on. This distinction is what Allen would classify within the textual, inter-textual and ideological codes of soap operas. He argues that these codes distinguish between different kinds of soap operas, depending on their specific textual characteristics, their inter-textual connection with other texts, and the body of beliefs and practices that are mobilized and appropriated by a specific text. To some extent this is also what Feuer classifies as the ritualistic and ideological approach to genre recognition, placing the specific text in a niche based on the relations that the text establishes between the audience and the text, and the larger body of cultural practices with which the text is related. From this perspective, it is possible to claim that some of the soap operas are religious while others are social, and so on.[13]

A good example of this distinction within serialized programs is found in the serials *The Sword of Tipu Sultan* and *Mahabharat*. The latter is a serial program that is based on a religious epic of the Hindu tradition. The narrative is based on the epic of the same name, where all aspects of the text reproduce the conventions of Hinduism. The text appropriates its representation of key characters from the existing descriptions of the Gods and Goddesses in a variety of interrelated Hindu texts. In *Mahabharat*, the characters are expected to speak in Hindi, and use costumes that are reminiscent of the illustrations in Hindu mythological texts. In the case of *The Sword of Tipu Sultan*, the signifying strategies reproduce the representations found in Islamic tradition, closer in form to the history textbook depiction of the struggles of Tipu Sultan—a Muslim king—against the British. These two texts can be classified as religious and historic serials based on the textual and inter-textual codes that align them with two different religions and narratives. While *Mahabharat* remains embedded within the mythology of Hinduism, the story of Tipu Sultan is based on the history of the struggle of the Muslim monarchs against British colonialism. This represents the finer distinction between the variety of serials, based primarily on the always-already texts that the serials mobilize and appropriate from. Finally, both the serials are semiotically similar to the textual tradition of Hindi films. In these serials,

[13] It is important to note here that this is not a classification based on content alone, but on the relation of the text with other texts from which it might have appropriated.

there is a good amount of melodrama, violence, romance and playback singing.

However, given the lack of any necessary and mechanistic principle in drawing these distinctions, it is argued that it is indeed difficult to precisely categorize a text as religious, social, political or pro-development. This ambiguity is also most evident in the case of *Mahabharat*. There is an informal body of argument that claims *Mahabharat* is not necessarily a religious text; on the contrary, it is a social documentary on a Hindu way of life. However, some authors, such as Chidananda Das Gupta, have argued that the serial has recoded the original Mahabharat text in such a way that it highlights its Hinduness more than its secular social commentary. I tend to agree with this position, since a close analysis of Mahabharat text shows that the fundamental dialectic in the serial is between the Hindu notions of evil and good. This is elaborated in the following chapters where I examine the text in depth to demystify some of the naturalized ideological positions of the text. It is also this ambiguity that makes the Mahabharat text an attractive center around which to develop an analysis of Doordarshan and its role and position in India's popular culture. This text has been able to capture the audience unlike any other serial on Doordarshan. Its popularity needs to be examined not only in terms of the text, but in relation to a variety of other cultural practices that have emerged during its broadcast. One such practice is the growing sense of a Hindu nation, and a growing Hindu awareness across India, where the hegemony of the Hindu faction has become increasingly oppressive. In view of this, it is useful to examine *Mahabharat* in depth, and understand the characteristics of this text and how it could have reproduced a variety of cultural, religious and social practices.

This is the task of textual analysis, where the aim is to understand the characteristics of a particular television text in terms of its primary textual and narrative strategies, and then in terms of its relation with other texts and the practices that it represents, and those that surround it. In the following chapters, I shall take a closer look at the Mahabharat to answer the questions posed in the first chapter about the position and relation of Doordarshan to a variety of cultural practices in India.

Summarizing briefly, the variety of programs on Doordarshan can be classified in a number of ways, using preexisting lists or modes of classification based on structural similarity and dissimilarity. I have chosen to concentrate primarily on the questions of education and entertainment, using this structural binary opposition as the key contradiction between programs on Doordarshan. This permits the reconsideration of a variety of programs as belonging to two broad genres of programming. Yet this classification is based on the textual and intertextual characteristics of the programs rather than on a content-based consideration. It is the structural relationship between programs that establish the distinction between programs and the similarity among programs. I would argue that this is the key to classification and the foundation for the analysis of specific programs. Such considerations allow me to claim that *Mahabharat* lies in an ambiguous position within the genre of serialized programs. It is this ambiguity of *Mahabharat* that also makes it particularly important to examine it in depth. Indeed, *Mahabharat's* ambiguity suggests the mediational role that the serial can play in establishing a connection between the social and religious practices. *Mahabharat* also represents a primary and popular corpus of text on Doordarshan, and this provides the rationale to look primarily at *Mahabharat* and then at other programs to understand Doordarshan. A reexamination of *Mahabharat*, its narrative structure, the signifying practices, the textual characteristics and the organizing codes permits the passage towards placing *Mahabharat* within the cultural formation of television, and then expanding the analysis to understanding Doordarshan itself. The fundamental assumption in this endeavor is that culture, cultural practices and cultural formations do not work in a vacuum, but are related to each other, and it is important to carefully select one of these elements and then examine it in relation to the others to begin to understand the chain of equivalences that make up popular culture. Consequently, *Mahabharat* needs to be examined as a text with its own distinct characteristics, and then in terms of the other entertainment and educational texts on television, and further, in relation to artefacts, formations and practices within the cultural arena of India.

# 4

# Mahabharat on Doordarshan

*'Maha' means great, and 'Bharat' is the name of
the first ruling family of India—its real historical
fact transformed into myth. It's the story of India,
the story of the World. It's our story as well, because
it's the story of a struggle.*

**Peter Brook,** *producer of the television play*
***The Mahabharata,*** *in the introduction to the
play that was aired on PBS in January 1991*

## The Ambiguities of Mahabharat
## on Doordarshan

**Of all the programs** discussed in the earlier chapter, perhaps the
most popular ones belong to the category that has often been
called the 'religious soap operas', particularly *Mahabharat* and
*Ramayan*.[1] As I had pointed out in the previous chapter, it is

[1] When it concluded in July 1990, a newspaper poll in India reported that, during
the airing of the ninety-three episode long serial of the *Mahabharat*, nearly 92 per
cent of the Indian television viewers were watching the serial. This was a greater
level of attention than what was attached with the viewing of the earlier religious
mythological soap opera, *Ramayan*, or with any other television program in India.
While these numbers are obtained through processes of survey analysis, with their
statistical biases, they suggest a reasonably high level of popularity for the particular
serialized soap opera.

difficult to conclusively label programs on Doordarshan into well-defined generic categories. The problem is connected to the way in which genre can be understood, as well as the ways in which programs have developed in India. When genre is considered in terms of norms of signification, with the repetitive use of similar visual signs and codes, some programs on Doordarshan can be combined into one set. On the other hand, when genre is conceptualized as the various syntactic combinations of various semantic units, a new set of categories emerge on Doordarshan.[2] I would argue that to examine *Mahabharat* in relation to the other programs on television, it is important to examine the variety of programs on Doordarshan from both these perspectives.

First, I shall focus on a specific narrative norm. In India, there is a large range of programs that use serialization as a key normative narrative style. These programs can be classified into two groups. First, there are programs that have one story serialised over a long period of time in which the stars play the same role over the entire serial. These programs are generically close to the soap opera of Western television. Secondly, there are programs that use the same set of stars in a series of episodes that use similar stories in every episode, the stars playing different roles in different telecasts. One example of such a program is *Chehere*, which examined the changing position of women in Indian society. The program used the same set of stars in a series of short stories adapted for television. There are thus two kinds of programs on Doordarshan that use the notion of serialization, which is a common presentational style for Indian television. This develops the necessary expectations in the viewer about the program, as well as defines the limits of the programs as serialized programs, as distinct from non-repetitive broadcasts such as television plays and talk shows.

These two kinds of serialized programs can also be examined in terms of the semantic units that are shared by them and the syntactic connections that compose the narrative. On one hand, there is a class of programs, (such as *Hum Log* and *Buniyaad*) which are family melodramas with a large set of characters placed

[2] These are the points made by Neale (1990) and Altman. Neale argues in his recent essay in *Screen* that genres need to be understood as processes of repetition, albeit with differences, variations and changes. Altman (1987) has argued that genres need to be considered as a combination of similar semantic units into similar syntactic chains.

in interconnected domestic situations. These programs use a continuing story about a set of people in a family, placing them in relations with each other, and with society. These are family stories in the sense Schatz (1981) conceptualizes the family unit made up of principal characters (such as the father, mother, husband and wife). The programs on Doordarshan are not very different from the genre of 'family melodrama' of the fifties Hollywood. In elaborating on this genre, both Schatz (1981) and Elsaesser (1986) point out that there are recognizable narrative strategies that distinguish the family melodrama of post-War Hollywood from other movies of that time. These distinguishing features include strategies such as dramatic discontinuity, the setting of stories in middle class American homes and concentration on the point of view of the victim. These repetitive features of the genre are the semantic units that are combined into syntactic chains.[3] These represent specific signs, (such as attire and setting,) that are connected together in similar ways to tell a story. The concern here is with the form of the narrative, and not its content.

Similarly, in the case of a large number of serialized programs on Doordarshan, there are semantic units and syntactic connections that produce specific narrative structures. These use similar reproductions of characters, events and actions to recount stories that are essentially tales of conflict between the progressive and reactionary social forces. Within this framework, the stories deal with issues that are contested in the social arena of India, (for instance, those that concern the position of women in society). Moreover, in the narrative structure, notions of 'good' and 'bad' are often produced around a set of signs that are connected with elements in the social space. For example, the setting of these narratives is often in middle class north Indian homes, which is often produced as 'good' social space, as opposed to the 'bad' space of a five-star hotel, where 'bad' things happen. Thus the narrative units, and their combination, concentrate on social elements and practices, as distinct from religious ones. Consequently, these programs can be conceptualized as 'social' programs.

On the other hand, *Ramayan* is perhaps the best example of a

---

[3] This is not to suggest that these are unchanging building blocks of narrative. On the other hand, the recombination and transformation of semantic units lead to the changes in genres, and the evolution of new genres. However, it is useful to recognize these evolving sets of narrative units to better understand the position of a narrative among a larger set of stories.

Doordarshan program that is predominantly concerned with a large set of Hindu religious practices. However, *Ramayan* is not the only program that deals with questions of religion. Periodically, during specific holy occasions, there are television programs that represent a variety of religious practices. Religion, and religious practices, have constantly played a role on Doordarshan. However, *Ramayan* was the first program that serialized an Indian epic, where the primary character is a Hindu incarnation, and brought it to the entire nation as a soap opera. The distinguishing factor for such programs lies in the semantic units that make up the genre. Most often, these include Hindu Gods and incarnations pitched in battle against the forces of irreligion. Structurally, these narrative units are most often engaged in a battle between the 'good' and the 'evil' forces which are characterized as religious elements and practices, as distinct from the social ones of the 'social' programs'.

In summary, the primary difference between social and religious programs is in the semantic units that make up the narrative. In the religious programs these units are overwhelmingly theological, concerned with the practices of the Hindu religion. On the other hand, social programs deal with practices that correspond with the social modes of behavior in everyday life. The primary similarity between these social and religious programs can be traced to the use of similar narrative strategies. Both set of programs use similar visual strategies (such as close-ups, shot/reverse shot, motivated editing, and background music). Programs on Indian television can, thus, be conceptualized in either of these two terms. Needless to say, these distinctions are not mutually exclusive, and a program can easily appropriate the signifying strategies of serialized broadcasts, but adopt a set of semantic units and syntactic combinations that make it difficult to identify it clearly as a religious or social program. *Mahabharat* was able to occupy that median position, where it co-opted from both the religious and the social. *Mahabharat* carved a position that lay somewhere between these two broad categories, co-opting liberally from the tradition of both the social and religious programs.

*Mahabharat* on Doordarshan incorporated a variety of religious and social practices, not necessarily distinguishing between the two. On the one hand, it represented practices that were central social concerns; on the other hand, it depicted practices that resembled Hindu rituals.

Among the issues that the television program *Mahabharat*

represents, one concerns the family and modes of interaction in the family. There are several episodes that deal with the issue of brotherly affection, duty to mother, and the role of the various members in a large family. For instance, when the eldest member of one the feuding families reminds his four brothers that he is ready to give up his entire empire for domestic peace, the camera captures him in a close up, collapsing the viewer and the four younger brothers, bringing home the significance of family loyalty in Indian society.

Yet this social relevance is always connected to the overwhelming Hinduness of the program. In episodes where a king is crowned, or a wedding takes place, the rituals are all Hindu. The priests on screen chant Hindu hymns and the deities being worshipped are recognizably Hindu. Further, one of the key characters in the television serial is Krishna—the Hindu incarnation who comes after Ram.[4] In these respects, particularly in the episodes which concentrate on Krishna, the serial comes closer to *Ramayan*.

*Mahabharat* is thus a social program in its elaborations on the models of social conduct. At the same time, it is religious in its depiction of the Hindu rituals of worship. In a way, the program begins to play a dual role, mediating between the religious and the social, and connecting the religious and social practices together in a continuous and interrelated chain.

To a large extent, this is precisely what happens in the opening sequence of every episode where the lyrics of the song in the signature section remind the viewer that the story of Mahabharat is of a conflict between the good and evil forces of society, where ultimately the good prevails.[5] The victory is attributed to an intrinsic power of the 'good', as well as the divine intervention of Krishna. This illustrates one of the ways in which the television program emphasizes its dual nature, playing on the notion of 'good' as a set of social practices which are also ideologically informed and underwritten by as a set of fundamental Hindu

[4] Within the Hindu system of belief, it is claimed that Ram and Krishna were two incarnations or 'avatars' of the Godhead Vishnu. Kinsley points this out saying, 'Earlier Hinduism considered Rama and Krishna "avatars" of Lord Vishnu' (Kinsley, 1982). They are considered to be 'supreme manifestations of divinity'.

[5] I will elaborate on this opening section later in this chapter. However, I shall use this section to make the point here that, in its narrative style, *Mahabharat* on Doordarshan, constantly underscores its dual effectivity.

religious concerns. By making the point in the signature section of each of the ninety-three episodes, the duality of *Mahabharat* on Doordarshan is maintained in all the broadcasts.

One consequence of this duality is the distancing of Mahabharat from Ramayan. The latter was primarily concerned with the Vishnu theology. Therefore, the story of Mahabharat is not necessarily read in the way that Ramayan was. Mahabharat is considered to be more of a story about India, an ideal India or '*Bharat*'. Similarly, the characters in Mahabharat are all human, with their human characteristics. Kinsley suggests this in his study of the cultural aspects of Hinduism. He says:

> The characters in Mahabharat seem more human, more given to flaws and shortcomings, than the heroes of Ramayan, and much of the appeal of the former stems from the characters, perplexities concerning the proper course of action in given circumstances (Kinsley, 1982).

This excerpt from Kinsley suggests that it is indeed difficult to describe the characters, and the story of Mahabharat, in a primarily religious way, but it is important to recognize the ambiguity of the story.

The ambiguity has also resulted in a mystification of the fundamental tension in the story. The dominant and central reading of the story is as a parable of a set of fundamental human values and practices. As the introduction to one literary version of the epic suggests:

> The story of this epic passed on to the coming generations through tradition having been told and retold down the ages. Full of ideal romance, mystery, thrills, suspense, chivalry, adventure, awe-inspiring exploits and spine chilling miracles, this wonderful epic depicts the moral as well as social values of the time and thus provides valuable guidance to the common householder for leading a pious, plain and virtuous life (Bhanot, 1990).

This citation exposes the dominant reading of the story as a set of moral and social values that informs the everyday life of Indians. There is no acknowledgment of the struggles between good and evil, which is the central theme of Mahabharat. The struggle has been reproduced in terms of a family feud. And it is this story of the feud between the Pandavas and the Kurus that has been naturalized as the primary Indian epic.

The ambiguity thus sets it apart from other programs on Indian television. It is difficult to categorize *Mahabharat* and place it in a self-contained niche. It could not be called a 'Soap Opera of the Gods' as unproblematically as *Ramayan* was named. Yet this elusive tale of Mahabharat remains a central one in Indian culture. Its very name suggests it is a story of India. (*maha* means great, *bharat* means India), crucial in thinking of India, and transforming the very image of India in its narrative.

In all the telling of Mahabharat, it becomes clear that the tale of Mahabharat occupies a central role in Indian culture. The importance of the story of Mahabharat in Indian culture is exposed in the words of Rajagopalachari:

> In this ancient and wonderful epic of our land there are many illustrative tales and sublime teachings, besides the narrative of the fortunes of the Pandavas. The Mahabharat is in fact a veritable ocean containing countless pearls and gems. It is, with the Ramayan, a living fountain of the ethics and culture of our Motherland (Rajagopalachari, 1989).

Here, the author highlights the importance of the story in thinking of India. However, the author refers to the story of Mahabharat, not as any particular textual artefact, but in a broader, more diffused and general sense. Indeed, the circulation of Mahabharat has been through a variety of discourses. Brook also points to this in saying:

> I heard it [the story of *Mahabharat*] the way Indians do, because Indians have been hearing the *Mahabharat* from their parents and story-tellers in bazaars, in temples, for over two thousand years. It's their great national epic; longer than the Bible, far longer than the *Homer*. To tell the whole story would take at least a year (Brook, 1991, from his introduction to the serial, *Mahabharat*, produced by him and aired on American Public Television).

Brook also suggests that the Mahabharat is the 'great national epic' of India, which is not necessarily located in any privileged text, but has circulated in a variety of texts.

Among these texts, the most recent appropriation by television has not necessarily changed the fundamental aspects of the story in any way, but has presented the story yet another time, now recoded on television. In doing so, the television serial has also become a central and popular program in India, albeit of ambiguous generic distinction. The television serial *Mahabharat* has also appropriated from all the various texts in which the story of the *Mahabharat* has been circulated in the popular culture.

## The Many Mahabharat Texts

The large body of texts through which the story of the Mahabharat has been circulated include the literary written word, the oral tradition of story-telling, the folk and rural tradition of *yatra* and village plays, the proscenium theater and film. As Kinsley points out, the Hindu epic Mahabharat was composed in Sanskrit between B.C. 400 to A.D. 400. This can be considered to be the source of all future renderings of this story. Through the centuries, the story of the Mahabharat has been handed down in the form of thousands of Sanskrit couplets, as a part of the larger universe of Hindu holy books such as the Vedas, Upanishads and the Ramayan.[6] All these texts have been a part of Indian popular culture of centuries. However, the stories from the Mahabharat and Ramayan have been appropriated into a variety of other discourses while the Vedas and the Upanishads remained primarily within the centers of Hindu theology.

The story of the Mahabharat has now been adapted into story books, children's comic books, village plays and film. The fundamental conflicts and tensions in the story have been retained in all the various cultural reproductions of the story. And the television producers were able to draw from this rich cultural stock to produce

[6] It is also important to remember that these books also represent a variety of changes in Hindu religious thinking. The Vedas represent a formative period of Hindu religion (2500 to 800 B.C.), the Upanishads a speculative period (800 to 400 B.C.) and the Mahabharat and Ramayan the epic period (400 B.C. to A.D. 400).

the serialized television program based on the Mahabharat epic. *Mahabharat* on Doordarshan appropriated liberally from these other renderings of the story and recoded the story of the Mahabharat for television, retaining the fundamental tale of the Mahabharat , but telling it in a style that is specific to television. The narrative style of television is understood as the process by which a story is told, in terms of the norms and codes of television (for instance, in the use of sounds and pictures). It is also these factors that make *Mahabharat* an ambiguous program with both social and religious significance. Thus, the specificity of television is intimately tied to the ways in which there has evolved specific ways of reproducing a story on television.

The specificity of *Mahabharat* on Doordarshan is manifest in two related factors: the conditions of production and the resulting serialization. Because of the serialization, a set of repetitive factors, emerge such as the recognizable faces who play the various roles, and the repetitive introductory and concluding sections for each episode. Furthermore, each episode in the serial uses the same combination of sets, costumes and props to bring the story to the small screen. Repetition also develops a sense of expectation in the viewer as the genre evolves as a corpus of programs on television that uses distinct signifying practices. All these factors ultimately play a role in redefining the position of the serial in the popular culture, and its connection with a larger set of practices in the popular culture.

## The Specificity of Mahabharat on Doordarshan

### The Conditions of Production

Television serials in India are produced by three collaborators who share power unequally to bring a serial to the viewer. These are the government, a financier and a television producer. Among them, the decision to air a program rests with the people at Mandi House—the name of the building which houses the administrative offices of the government that control decisions regarding Doordarshan.

Typically, the process involves several steps. First, a producer and a financier cooperate to produce a set of television pilots. These pilot programs are then reviewed by the decision makers at Mandi House. If the serial is approved, the financier provides the funds to produce a fixed number of serials. These serials are then aired over a period of time.

These steps are the result of the partial commercialization of television in India. Following the success of the ASIAD telecast in 1982, there was a strong drive to open the financing of Doordarshan to private funds. However, in order to retain control of what goes on the air, Mandi House ensured that they would have the final say in the programs that are produced with external resources. These programs are thus distinct from programs that are produced by Doordarshan, using funds available through license fees and the commercial spots aired on television. Based on their conditions of production, there are two broad kinds of programs that can be identified: programs that are produced and financed by Doordarshan and, externally produced and externally funded programs. The former includes news programs and talk shows, while the latter are predominantly entertainment programs.

Noticeably, this is the same break between education and entertainment that I have discussed earlier. The distinction between education and entertainment is indeed an ambiguous one. However, the significance of this uncertain distinction lies in the fact that the producer has to be careful to create a product that will not only gain the sponsorship of a financier, but will also have to be ideologically acceptable to the decision makers at Mandi House. Decisions at Mandi House are influenced by a variety of concerns which can be summarized in the maxim: television should not promote 'cheap' entertainment but should telecast programs that have some didactic value. These ambiguous terms are the ones that distinguish between entertainment and educational programs— the former being 'cheap'. This has also resulted in the airing of serials that can claim some effectivity in addition to entertainment. For instance, non-religious soap operas like *Buniyaad* and *Hum Log* claimed to be serials that highlighted 'national integration', given their pro-development emphasis.

The didactic concern is also connected with the cultural, political and social practices that are to be represented in the program. By selecting programs that reproduce the ideologically preferred practices, the government is constantly attempting to circulate a set of dominant images, for instance those of 'nation', 'national culture' and 'national integration'.[7] In other words, programs are expected to reconstruct a national image, and 'teach' the viewer to become an ideal Indian.

From these perspectives, the consecutive approval for *Ramayan* and *Mahabharat* indicate the ruling religious connections that are being reproduced in India now—around a Hindu center. In this process of selection, the State and the ruling party, through Mandi House, is able to maintain control, and determine what is circulated on television.

This is perhaps the first time that the story Mahabharat has been reproduced by a social bloc who are in a position to exercise cultural power by their control over the television medium. The television serial is unlike the circulation of the story in other modes (for example, the literary and oral modes in which there is always the need to retell the story in a language specific to the region of the country). Doordarshan, however, could bring a 'standardized' story, simultaneously, to a large part of the country in one language. While Doordarshan gained purchase over India's popular culture, the sponsor and the producer were able to reap substantial profits by serialising *Mahabharat*.

The producer also found it more profitable to serialize the story on television. This is because the financier is often more willing to finance a program that will stay on the air for a longer period of time, thus offering the financier a prolonged exposure to the viewer. Thus it was to Godrej's advantage to sponsor a large number of episodes, since it made the company visible for a longer period of time. At the beginning of every episode, there would be a sixty second spot that would remind the viewer that the epic was being brought to them by Godrej.[8] Thus there was enough motivation to prolong the story.

Finally, the sponsors chose a story that was so long it could only be told in a serial fashion. Mahabharat is made up of nearly eighty-three thousand couplets divided into eighteen cantos. This story could be brought to television only in the form of a serial.

---

[7] The question of nation, nationhood and national culture, in relation to *Mahabharat* on Doordarshan, are dealt with in a later chapter.

[8] Godrej manufactures a variety of products from soap to refrigerators.

Consequently, a significant aspect of *Mahabharat* on Doordarshan is its serialization into a set of episodes.

## Serialization of Mahabharat on Doordarshan

Serialising a story results in dividing up the narrative into multiple episodes. Each episode lays the foundation for the following one. In most cases, each episode ends with a narrative situation that motivates the next episode. There is usually no clear indication of the end of the serial. Both in the West and India, soap operas have primarily been serialized programs. Episodes in serials such as *Hum Log* in India, and *General Hospital* in America, are narrated in such a way that it appears as if the narrative will never end. These narratives continue without closure, where each episode will have some conclusions, but there is rarely any necessary 'end' to the soap opera story, except when the series is concluded. This was the case with the Indian serialized programs such as *Buniyaad* and *Hum Log*, where there was an initial contract between the producer, sponsor and Doordarshan, that there would be a fixed number of episodes. The conclusion of the serial after the airing of the contracted number of episodes is also the last time the viewer ever gets to see the serial, unless the serial is re-aired under syndication. Since Doordarshan is still predominantly a single channel system, there is no way in which the serial can be syndicated on a second channel, as is often the case with American serials.

These aspects of serialization also hold true for *Mahabharat* on Doordarshan. However, in the case of *Mahabharat* (and *Ramayan*) there is an additional factor that needs to be considered. The Mahabharat story existed in the cultural stock of India, and there was a well-defined conclusion to the tale. As I have mentioned earlier, the story of the Mahabharat has been circulated in a variety of texts for centuries. The story has become central to Indian culture, and it is not an exaggeration to claim that nearly everyone in India is familiar with the Mahabharat and its centrality in Indian life. In some ways the Mahabharat is the ancient history of India, a recounting of Indian religious, social and cultural practices. The age-old story has been brought back to television, where it has been recoded and replotted and serialized. However, it is unlike *Hum Log* or *Buniyaad*—the two other most notable serialized programs to be aired on Doordarshan. In the case of these programs, the end was a surprise and, as some popular press indicated, a matter of dismay and disappointment too.[9] However, in the case of the Mahabharat and Ramayan, there is little that is unexpected in the story. *Mahabharat* on television only reiterates the already well-known story in the episodic language of television. This was, however, done very effectively, constantly generating in the viewer a desire to see what happens next, even though one might very well know what the next event will be. From the very first episode of the serial, most of the audience knew very well what was to follow, and what was to be the conclusion. Yet, television, by visualizing this historic epic and by making it available to the entire country, was able to regenerate an interest in this story, reemphasizing its centrality in Indian culture. This was possible because of serialization, and the way in which *Mahabharat* predictably returned every week and recaptured the viewer's attention. Serialization played on the expectations of the audience, as they waited patiently for their favorite part of the story to see that part come alive on television in the domesticity of their home.[10]

The primary significance of serialization thus lies in the way in which *Mahabharat* on Doordarshan was able to take a well known story, and bring it back to the audience every week. Doordarshan became a forum where the central tale of India was repeated every week, reemphasizing not only the centrality of Mahabharat but also redescribing the position of television. Doordarshan was no longer only a didactic tool, but a site where the stories of the Mahabharat were coming alive, brought to life by the familiar faces that played the lead roles. Serialization also produced the stars of *Mahabharat*.

### The Stars of *Mahabharat* on Doordarshan

'Religious soap opera' stars emerged as a result of the serialization of the story on television. It is in episodic programs on television

---

[9] This was primarily because the viewers developed a familiarity with the characters; and newspaper reports (*Telegraph*) described how there was a general disappointment when the familiar characters were not available periodically. The space opened by these serials was adequately filled by the *Mahabharat* and *Ramayan* programs.

[10] I will be developing on this issue, later in this work when I discuss the way in which television in India is related to domestic time and space.

that faces become recognizable, and anticipated. In precisely that way, the unknown people who portrayed the characters in *Mahabharat* became worshipped icons in a short time, as they returned to millions of homes every Sunday as Arjun, Krishna or Draupadi.

For example, the person who played Ram in *Ramayan* was worshipped as an incarnation by some people in the village of Umbergaon, where the serial was shot. People would fall at his feet when he appeared in public, collapsing the actor and the personality of Ram into one. Such was the power of the serial.

Similarly, the actress who portrayed Draupadi in *Mahabharat* received a lot of unpleasant publicity for wearing Western style dresses. This was considered unbecoming of a person who comes home to millions of viewers as Draupadi—the ideal Hindu woman.

Finally, the actor who plays Arjun in *Mahabharat* chose to change his Muslim name to a show business alias of 'Arjun', not only hiding his religion but collapsing his off-screen name with the character he portrays. At the end of each serial, a still picture of every individual is displayed with their name super-imposed— Arjun's face comes up, with the name Arjun. At that instant, there is a closure between the 'real' person and the character in the narrative.

These stars make the television rendering of *Mahabharat* different from other production of the epic. In film, theater and *yatra* there is little sense of continuity either of narrative, or of the people who play the roles of the characters in the narrative.[11] However, television soap operas are generically known for the redundancy of characters and their recurrence every week. This happened in the case of the television program *Mahabharat* too. Consequently, nowhere else but on television did the ideal Hindu woman—Draupadi—have the same recognizable face week after week.

Moreover, these actors and actresses had little semiotic baggage to carry with them when they started to play the part of Krishna, Draupadi or Arjun. Most of the stars were chosen from a fresh pool of applicants and, often, the selected faces had not appeared on media before. This signifies that the face that was associated with Arjun, Draupadi or Krishna had not been in the public forum before and had entered the semiotic space of television free of any earlier connection with any other character.

[11] There are, however, exceptions, for instance in the case of the Bond movies, or in the case of the formulaic Hindi movies which repeatedly use similar story lines.

The pool of actors on serials such as *Mahabharat* usually does not overlap with the large number of film stars. Consequently, the people who acted in the *Mahabharat* serial were unlike the film stars who had played the parts of Arjun and others in the film version of *Mahabharat*. The latter were established stars, and had a history of stardom. When they play a character in *Mahabharat*, the viewer would first relate the face to a star, and then to the role he or she plays. For instance, the film version of *Mahabharat* is often remembered as the one where Dara Singh plays Bhim. The implication is in the expectation that a heavyweight champion turned film star, like Dara Singh, would play the role of the biggest and strongest of the five Pandava brothers. When film stars cross into television space, they bring such histories with them. However, in the case of *Mahabharat* on Doordarshan, there were few such crossovers, and the key roles were played by new faces that soon became connected to the characters they played. No doubt,this made the characters much more palpable to the viewer. This was possible only on television.

The identity of the stars and their fictional roles were further collapsed in the repetitive use of the signature section at the beginning of every episode, and the credits section at the end of the episodes. Here, the pictures and stills reiterated the connection between the faces and the characters. Thus Arjun in the narrative, and Arjun the actor, were inseparable. The introductory and concluding sections of each episode also reiterated a set of fundamental issues that recurred in the serial. Thus, serialization not only produced stars but also attached a repetitive opening and closing section to each episode.

## The Signature Section of *Mahabharat* on Doordarshan

Serialized programs on television often have an initial section that is repeated at the beginning of every episode. This serves a variety of purposes. First, it offers familiar visual images that become necessarily connected to the particular serial. This phenomenon is best understood in terms of genre as process, where certain aspects of the program become normative and expected. In serialized programs on television, it is expected that there will be a section that will provide the frame for the episode. The opening and closing sections thus mark the limits of the episode within the flow of television. Secondly, the signature section in *Mahabharat* provided the framework within which the serial was to be placed, to facilitate the reading of any episode. In a way, the opening and closing section thus become the markers for the limits of the episode in terms of the semantic units that it deals with. If offers the narrative boundaries for the entire serial, pointing out, as in the case of *Mahabharat*, that it is a story of a Hindu India, and *bharat*, thus excluding the possibility of it being a story of any other alternative imaging of India, where religion is not central. Thus it provides the outlines, or the super-text, for reading the episode and the serial. Finally, this section also becomes an internal audience; it provides the viewer a cue for the preferred and expected reading of the text.[12] For these reasons, it is crucial to examine this section of the serialized programs carefully.

The episodes of *Mahabharat* on Doordarshan begin with the logo 'B.R. TV', representing the producers of the serial. This is followed by the signature section.[13] The signature section begins with a shot of a battlefield, where elephant-riding warriors are engaged in battle. This represents the ultimate conflict on the battlefields of Kurukshetra. Over the sound of cymbals and armor, the voice-over repeats the word 'Mahabharat' three times, each time, the word appearing on the screen, superimposed on the picture of the battlefield. The first time the word is spelt out in Hindi, then in English, and finally in Urdu. This represents the two languages that are articulated with the primary religions in India—Hinduism and Islam. English, of course, remains the language that a large part of India uses and understands.

This is followed by the credits. The credits are presented both in English and Hindi, superimposed over pictures that remind the viewer of countless similar illustrations and paintings that have accompanied the story of the Mahabharat. From comic books to voluminous Sanskrit texts, all have used similar illustrations to illuminate the story of the Mahabharat. This further forges the generic connection between religion and the television serial. While the credits continue, there is a voice-over that reemphasizes the

[12] For instance, in the case of the serial *Ramayan*, this was further underscored by the appearance of Ashok Kumar, a notable film star, who offered an interpretive commentary at the end of each of the episodes.

[13] I call this a 'section' because it is longer and more elaborate than a simple signature tune and opening sequence of shots.

fundamental aspect of the story—the need for divine incarnations like Krishna to arrive on earth in order to resolve the conflict between the forces of good and evil.

At the end of the credits, the picture dissolves to a shot of the universe and a disembodied voice—the voice of 'time'—offers the viewer a short introduction to the serial, helping to place the particular episode in relation to the preceding episodes.

Following this, the episode begins, and continues for nearly thirty-five minutes.

At the end of the episode a set of credits reappear, and these are superimposed on still pictures of the various actors and actresses as their names appear at the bottom of the screen, spelled out in Hindi and English. The closing of each episode is marked by a song that provides the background for the word 'Mahabharat', now spelled out in nine different Indian scripts. The closing song reminds the viewers that they have been watching the story of *bharat*, a homage to the heroes, a story that never grows old, and which is relevant to our lives today as Indians. The song is followed by the word 'Mahabharat' and the episode number.

The significance of the opening and closing section is intimately tied to the notion of serialization. This section of the broadcast constantly reminds the viewer of the fundamental concerns of the television show in terms of the struggles the serial depicts and the final inevitable resolution of the tension. While every episode expands on these themes, the kernel of the Mahabharat story is recounted every time in the opening and closing sequences.

Serialization has made it possible to bring these images recurrently into the Indian home. In no other rendering of the epic is there such a structured section that repeats the same issues in every narration. Because of this, serialization is fundamental to the reproduction of the Mahabharat on television. It has not only brought the story to the Indian viewer every week, but has used a set of familiar faces, images and music to reemphasize a preferred reading of the story of the Mahabharat.

Serialization, thus, results in familiarizing the viewer with a variety of aspects of the story, including the fundamental tensions in the story and the faces that bring the story to life. However, the specificity of *Mahabharat* on Doordarshan goes beyond the issue of serialization. Not only has Doordarshan been able to bring the story back over and over again, but it has been able to reproduce the story in a way that the Doordarshan rendering becomes much more powerful than the other telling of the Mahabharat. This has partly been achieved in the way Doordarshan repetitively captured the geographic setting of the story, with its details of costume, language and music.

## Sets, Costumes and Props for *Mahabharat* on Doordarshan

The geographic setting of the epic is in and around the ancient city of Hastinapur. The city, and the surrounding Gangetic plains, is carefully reproduced in the television serial. Hastinapur has always been recognized to be somewhere in northern India, within the large fertile Gangetic plains. Moreover, this part of the country is also recognized as the birthplace of other prominent Indian religious personalities such as Ram, earlier portrayed in the soap opera *Ramayan*, and Krishna, who plays a prominent role in the *Mahabharat*.[14] This geographic area of India is now characterized as the Hindi-Hindu belt of India, where the language is predominantly Hindi, and the population predominantly Hindu. In the television serial, northern India is reproduced as historical India, one that stands for the preferred image of 'bharat' or India. The television program captures this setting in detail, particularly in the location shots.

The broadcast also accentuates the setting by the costumes of the people who inhabit Hastinapur. Here I refer more to the dresses of the common people who are sometimes portrayed in the episodes. These are people who dress as rural north Indians of the Gangetic plains do. Dress establishes a link between the preferred practices of attire, and a geographic location. It also has a religious connotation. By depicting a farmer in Hastinapur wearing a 'dhoti', a set of connections are being drawn between the apparel of the north Indian farmer and the preferred image of rural India.

In the use of costumes for the principal characters, the television

[14] This is also the site of the current controversy over the location of the birthplace of Ram. The political party in India that is closest in its alliance with the Hindu fundamentalist groups have made this controversy the focus of their election campaign. The argument is over an Islamic mosque that evidently stands on the very site where Lord Rama was born in the north Indian village of Ayodhya—claimed to be close to legendary Hastinapur too.

serial appropriates from a variety of sources. North Indian representations of the royal attire, crown, and other such details of
dress have been meticulously reproduced from old illustrations
and paintings. Noticeably, these illustrations and paintings are
reproductive of a north Indian tradition of the Mahabharat. By
appropriating from these illustrations, the serial is not only able to
establish the inter-textual relation between the traditional renderings of the Mahabharat, but with a selective tradition that is
representative of a linguistic and regional preference.

Concurrently, there is an appropriation from the stage, folk
plays and film, which have also used the older illustrations as their
sources. The television rendering uses all these sources to reproduce
an image of the characters that is well recognizable in a variety of
discourses ranging from comic books to the television genre of
religious serialized programs, particularly *Ramayan* .

The significance of the use of a specific set of costumes, props
and backdrops in all the episodes lies primarily in the way that the
serial is able to reproduce and circulate a particular ethnic representation of the characters. In spite of the variety of traditions of
attire available in India, there is a constant attempt to appropriate
from a specific north Indian tradition. This process is specific to
the television rendering of the Mahabharat. In other reproductions
of the story, regional practices are reproduced in the telling of the
Mahabharat. For example, when the Mahabharat is read in a
temple gathering in West Bengal, it is read in Bengali, and in the
folk plays of Bengal the people dress in traditional Bengali attire.
However, on television, the Mahabharat was standardized into a
depiction that ended up appropriating from north India and, in its
National Network, Doordarshan constantly circulated this specific
rendering. In short, the Mahabharat was universalized and naturalized into a north Indian story on Doordarshan. This was further
facilitated by the choice of the language of the broadcast and the
overall use of sound and music.

### The Use of Sound in *Mahabharat* on Doordarshan

*Mahabharat* on Doordarshan constantly borrowed the language
and music of a preferred region of India. The language of the
broadcast is not the pedestrian Hindi of Bombay, but a precise and
refined Hindi that is representative of a small section of north-
central India, particularly around the area which is considered to

be the childhood playground of Krishna. This draws the connection between the language, Hinduism and northern India, not only positioning *Mahabharat* within the ongoing language tensions in India, but also placing the medium of television in a specific position with respect to these struggles.

Similarly, in the use of music, a selection process has emerged through which a particular kind of music and dance has been appropriated into the serial.[15] The music that has been used in *Mahabharat* is characteristically north Indian. However, the use of music has also drawn a set of inter-textual connections between *Mahabharat* on Doordarshan and the other texts that surround it in the popular cultural space.

In some ways, the use of music on Indian television is not very different from the use of music in Indian film. The primary reason for this is the strong influence of cinema on television. The producer of *Mahabharat* on Doordarshan is a veteran of the big screen, and so the use of music has been similar to the way it has been used in film. For example, the use of background music to develop a mood for a particular scene is common to both cinema and television. However, in the serialized narrative form of television, the background music also reminds the viewer constantly about particular moods associated with particular characters or events. For instance, whenever the conspiratorial character of Shakuni appears, there is sinister background music that reemphasizes the villainy of this character. Thus, music offers a commentary on the character, establishes the mood of a scene, and describes the role of the character in the narrative. In the episodic nature of television, the recurrent use of the tune reemphasizes the evil of Shakuni. Similarly, when Krishna or one of the Pandava brothers performs an act of valor, there is music in the background to underscore the goodness of the action. This is specific to television in the way it can repeat the same musical score in every episode. In films, a particular

---

[15] Music usually plays a key role in television soap operas. As Allen points out:

> Music can be used as an auditory signature, announcing each episode of a soap—a convention widely used in other types of television programming. Also, a piece of music can be associated with a particular character or relationship (Allen, 1985).

In a similar way, Altman (1986) points out various ways in which music provides labelling and italicizing what is important in the narrative. Such use of music is apparent in *Mahabharat* on Doordarshan too.

mood-music is used only within the limits of a specific movie. However, in television serials, because of the segmented and repetitive nature of the story, the same music returns in every episode, and in every opening sequence, thus constantly emphasizing the way a particular event or character should be understood. Music, therefore, also offers an on-going commentary and a connection between parts of the narrative.

Frequently, a short song offers a commentary, and an interpretation of a situation to facilitate a preferred reading of the text. Altman calls this music the internal audience. It is the ideal audience, giving the viewer cues on how the scene should be read. The song segment used frequently in the serial *Mahabharat*, also uses a well recognized tune from a Hindu religious song which glorifies the incarnation 'Jagadish'.[16] Further, this is sung using the Hindu *kirtan* tune—typical Hindu hymn music—forming yet another bridge between the television program and Hindu religious practices.

Moreover, a combination of song and dance play a part in the progression of the narrative, representing, for instance, a romantic situation, or a celebration. In this use of music, the characters are often engaged in an accompanying dance, where the music and dance, in combination, play a part in progressing the story. Typically, the choreographic form that has been used in the *Mahabharat* soap opera comes from the tradition of classical Indian dance, usually articulated with the temple dances. The choreographic style is used in temples, and in Hindu worship, to invoke the Gods. Here, too, a connection is drawn between what is represented as the preferred dance form among the many choreographic practices in India. It is those that are already articulated with the Hindu religion, as practiced in north and central India, that are used in the television rendering of *Mahabharat*. A dance form that was restricted to the temple and specialized dance performances was transformed by television into a popular cultural form. The adaptation of dance in the telling of the Mahabharat story, thus, not only transformed the narrative but also transformed the dance by circulating it across the nation, and making it a part of popular culture. The transformation of the choreographic style is thus similar to the way in which the stars were made familiar, and the

---

[16] Jagadish is another name for Ram.

settings, costumes props and Hindi were all circulated as the ones preferably connected with the Mahabharat.

Finally, the relationship between music and the *Mahabharat* serial on television becomes crucial because many of the characters in the tale have been used in other programs on television, where music has been able to emphasize the structural position of the character in the narrative. A good illustration is in the episodes that deal with the relationship between Krishna and his consort Radha. Their romantic relationship has been reproduced in dance dramas and musical programs on television. In addition, the short serial *Krishna*, based on the life of the incarnation, draws a semiotic connection between itself and the *Mahabharat* serial by focusing on the flute that Krishna plays. Here music, and the instrument, become the semiotic thread that not only ties the two serials together, but also reproduces the popular image of Krishna as the incarnation whose mastery of the flute is legendary in Indian popular culture.

These connections between the television serial and a set of larger elements in culture are significant because of the centrality of the Mahabharat in Indian popular culture. This popular story has now been reproduced on Doordarshan as the narrative of a family feud between two warring families. Yet, the opening and closing sequence of the episodes point out that the Mahabharat is also the story of a conflict between the forces of evil and good. Therefore, a connection is established between 'goodness' and the deeds of one family, consequently equating the activities of the other family with a lack of virtue. Furthermore, the everyday activities of the 'good' Pandava family correspond with the practices of specific social groups in India.

There is, therefore, an ongoing struggle in the television serial to constantly make a connection between an abstract struggle between good/evil, and a concrete struggle between two families, extrapolating to the struggle between a set of divergent cultural/ social practices. Television is able to make the connection in this serial because of the way in which television has been able to retell the Mahabharat story, using the signifying style of television. As I have pointed out earlier, it is the combination of the strategies of television, the ambiguity of the Mahabharat story and the centrality of the epic that makes the reproduction of this story on television so powerful. In circulating this mythological story on television,

Doordarshan was able to produce a central image of the medium in popular culture that no other program had been able to achieve before. This was possible not only because of the specificity of television, but also because the story of the Mahabharat is so powerful and well known. Thus it will be useful to take a brief look at some of the key aspects of the story.

## The Story of the Mahabharat: The Characters and Events

Needless to say, this is a mere gloss and it is indeed beyond the scope of this project to even summarize the epic. Here I am highlighting those issues that have a bearing on the understanding of the relation between the serial and the broader arena of popular culture.

In the Mahabharat story, the characters can be divided into three broad categories; the Gods, the demons and the mortals. This three-way grouping also represents the two fundamental opposing forces within the narrative—the Gods represent *dharma*, the demons represent *adharma* and the mortals are evenly distributed between these positions.[17]

As I have pointed out earlier, the voice over the credits at the beginning of every episode explains this opposition. The viewer is also reminded that there are times on earth when *adharma* becomes dominant and, at such times, God comes down to earth, as an incarnation, to weed out *adharma* and reestablish the rule of law or *dharma*. All characters occupy positions around this fundamental issue of an all-embracing struggle.

The two key sets of characters are the members of the Kuru and the Pandava families. A complicated genealogy is drawn up in the early part of the narrative where the origin of these two families is traced through convoluted paths. Dhritarashtra and Pandu emerge as the patriarchs of these two families. Dhritarashtra is the father of the hundred Kuru brothers. He is also the king of an empire that has its capital in Hastinapur.

Pandu, Dhritarashtra's brother, is the victim of a supernatural

---

[17] Dharma refers to the rule of law, a rule of goodness, and *adharma* to its opposite.

curse. Because of this, it is ordained that Pandu will fall dead if he is to have physical contact with any woman. This makes it necessary for Pandu's wives, Kunti and Madri, to invoke a supernatural blessing and have five children born out of divine intervention. Thus are born the five brothers: Yudhistir, born of the God of wisdom—Dharma; Bhim, born of the God of the winds—Vayu; Arjun, born of the king of the Gods—Indra; and their two twin brothers, Nakul and Shahadev, born of Aswini. These are the five Pandava brothers.

Because of their divine origin, each of the Pandava brothers represent particular foci of strength—the eldest becomes the oracle and keeper of *dharma*, the second, Bhim, becomes the strongest of the brothers, Arjun becomes the best archer, and the younger two become monuments of patience and virtue. These five brothers are represented as the paragons of virtue, and the deeds that they perform become articulated with all that is preferred and ideologically correct.

This is further strengthened by their alliance with Krishna—the incarnation—who is the Pandavas' chief ally, advisor and friend. Krishna is the incarnation who has alighted on earth to rid it of *adharma*. In numerous ways, Krishna underwrites the actions of the Pandava brothers as the preferred ones, within the discourse of *dharma*.

The other key family in the story are the Kurus. This family is hostile to the Pandavas. They are led by Dhritarashtra's eldest son Duryadhan. Across the entire narrative, this person has been depicted as the evil and deviant one. Every action of his is reproduced as oppositional to *dharma*, and his chief advisor—his maternal uncle, Shakuni (literal translation means 'vulture')—is the ideological antithesis of Krishna. In the text, Shakuni plays a crucial role as the person who constantly plans the destruction of the Pandavas.

The two key women in this story are Kunti, the mother of the Pandavas, and Draupadi, their wife. These two women, Kunti and Draupadi, are related to the Pandavas, and to Krishna. The women on the Kuru side of the family are relatively unimportant (Table 4.1).

In this epic, the families are positioned at opposite ends, where the fundamental opposition remains between good and evil, *dharma* and *adharma*. The conflict is concretized in the form of a

Table 4.1: *The Simplified Narrative Structure of* Mahabharat *and its Transformations*

---

**The conflict between**
good : evil
*dharma : adharma*

**concretized into a family feud**
Pandavas : Kurus

**composed of**

| | |
|---|---|
| Yudhistir: | Duryadhan |
| Bhim: | the Hundred |
| Arjun | Brothers |
| Nakul | |
| Shahadev | |
| *wife* – Draupadi | |
| *mother* – Kunti & Madri | |
| *father* – Pandu | |

**supported by**
Krishna : Shakuni

***resolved in the battle***
*of*
***Kurukshetra***
*where*
*the*
***Pandavas prevail***

***Thus dharma prevails***

---

family feud. In the end, the fundamental binary opposition between *dharma* and *adharma* is resolved in the battle of Kurukshetra. However, this binary opposition is not unambiguously evident. Indeed, as Kinsley points out, the story of the Mahabharat is not as unambiguous a conflict between good and evil as the Ramayan is. On the contrary, in popular culture, the Mahabharat is simply the story of a family feud, where two clans fight for control over the north Indian plains. For instance, this is what the preface to a children's comic book describes the 'Mahabharat' as: 'The epic narrates the story of the feud between the Kauravas and their cousins, the Pandavas' (Pai, 1988). Mystified within this conflict is the struggle between *dharma* and *adharma*, represented and mediated by the conflict between the various characters in the narrative.

In the story, *dharma* is represented by the activities of the

Pandavas. This has produced a popular discourse where the Pandavas stand for all that is good and preferred while the Kurus
represent all that is deviant, marginalized and destructive. For
instance, in Rajagopalachari's translation of the story into English,
he says:

> In a short time the Pandavas gained mastery over the Vedas and
> the Vedanta[18] as well as over the various arts, especially pertain-
> ing to the kshatriyas.[19] The Kauravas (Kurus), the sons of the
> blind Dhritarashtra, became jealous of the Pandavas and tried
> to injure them in various ways (Rajagopalachari, 1989).

Here the translator only reemphasizes that the Pandavas represent
the good in life while the Kurus are the evil ones.

The discourse around *dharma* is further strengthened in the
legend by other connections that are drawn in the narrative. The
term *dharma* not only depicts the rule of law and wisdom, but also
the God of wisdom and knowledge. Within the various magical
elements of the story, the birth of the eldest brother of the five
Pandavas is associated with the God of wisdom—Dharma. This
only emphasizes the already existing connection between the practices of the Pandavas, their divine origin and *dharma*.

The story of the Mahabharat thus emerges as a story of a
conflict, with an abstract deep structure to the conflict, which is
concretized in the narrative as a battle between two families. On
television this story was retold over ninety-three episodes, with
nearly all the television viewers watching it. The story was also
spread over a long period of time, with the beginning and end of
every episode repeatedly making the point that the serial is a story
of a fight between *dharma* and *adharma*. In this battle, the Pandavas
and the Kurus represent *dharma* and *adharma*, respectively. Meanwhile, the everyday material practices of the characters in the
serial were represented on television by the use of specific costumes,
the language Hindi, and particular music and dance. These practices
are all connected with a specific section of India. Consequently, it can
be argued that by approving the broadcast of this story on television,
the decision makers at Mandi House drew a correspondence between

[18] The two chief texts that embody the basic Hindu philosophy of religion.
[19] The warrior caste.

what is 'good' and the practices of the Pandavas, whose everyday activities reproduced the cultural, social and religious practices of the Hindu-Hindi belt of north India. These sets of connections define the role that this popular serial has played in positioning Doordarshan in the cultural space of India.

I shall now elaborate on this specific position by examining the way in which the struggles represented in the serial are connected with the ongoing tensions in India. After drawing these connections, it would also be possible to understand the role that television plays in redefining Indian popular culture.

However, to examine the connection between Mahabharat and Doordarshan, and the larger set of contradictory elements in popular culture, it is also necessary to consider the primary tensions in India today (for instance, those around language and religion) and then find the connection or 'articulation' between these straining forces. From then on, it is necessary to see how the story of the Mahabharat is able to mediate these tensions, and relate the conflicts in the story with a broader set of conflicts in a larger cultural and social space. This is the substance of the next chapter.

# 5

# Beyond *Mahabharat*: The Articulation of the Television Medium and Social Cultural Practices

> *What had been isolated as a medium, in many ways rightly as a way of emphasizing the material production which any art must be, came to be seen, inevitably, as social practice; or, in the crisis of modern cultural production, as a crisis of social practice.*
>
> **Raymond Williams**, *Marxism and Literature*

## Rethinking the Meaning of 'Contradictions'

**My contention, in** Chapter 4, was that *Mahabharat* on television is able to use a variety of narrative strategies that are specific to television in order to reproduce the well-known story in the cultural space of India. In replotting the tale, Doordarshan is also able to circulate a preferred set of practices as the dominant and 'good' practices in India[1] represented by the everyday life activities of the

---

[1] It is important to note that the term 'practices' here refers to a variety of ideas, including the everyday material activities of people, their religious rituals, language, regional modalities, gendered relationships, cultural activities, social relations and political inclinations. Needless to say, the term has to be understood in a variety of

Pandava family. Doordarshan also connects its specific retelling of the Mahabharat, particularly in the use of the signature section, the setting, music and language, with a set of ongoing struggles in India. For instance, by preferring to use a north Indian represent-ation of attire, *Mahabharat* on Doordarshan is able to prioritize that as the chosen and 'natural' representation of Indian rural dress.

The crucial issue here is to be able to map these connections between the television text and the ongoing struggles and contra-dictions in India. However, to do so, there are two prerequisites: first, to rethink the notion of contradiction itself and, secondly, to examine the continuing contradictions in India and then draw connections between the television text and the contradictions.

The notion of contradictions can be broken up into three con-ceptual parts. First, a contradiction is related with struggle. There are always forces in any society that are constantly struggling with each other to gain dominance over the other to obtain a position of leadership.[2] For example, there is an ongoing struggle in India over the question of linguistic domination. While north Indian hegemony is pushing hard to enforce Hindi as the national language, non-Hindi speaking areas of India are struggling against this. This struggle is the result of a contradiction over language. Similar struggles can be identified around questions of region, religion and so on.

The second way in which contradictions can be thought of concerns the notion of tension. For example, because of the contra-dictions around language, there is an ongoing struggle between linguistic groups and regions to oppose a north Indian leadership. This opposition is manifest in the form of tensions which results in political violence, military action or even a change of leadership. The contradictions that exist in Indian society manifest themselves

---

ways. When I refer to religious practices, most often it is in reference to the religious activities of a social bloc. It is these activities, or religious practices, that distinguish one religious faction from another. For example, Hindus do not eat beef, which represents a material activity whose relationship to Hinduism makes it not only a culinary habit but also a religious practice. While the word 'practice' has to be used carefully, its meaning also should be understood in a broad way.

[2] This is invoking Gramsci and his notion of hegemony. This is what I have discussed earlier, in Chapter 2, in rethinking culture as a set of practices that are struggling with each other to gain a position of leadership.

in factions that are struggling with each other, resulting in a variety of tensions, ultimately leading to social and cultural changes. Thus, when I speak of contradictions, I am also invoking the corresponding struggles and tensions.

Finally, contradictions are not unrelated. Indeed, various contradictions, struggles and tensions are related to each other. This relation is best conceptualized as a process of articulation where no necessary connections remain between the various contradictions, but connections are produced by the work of ideology.[3] Therefore, it is impossible to severe the connections between the contradictions in India. Consequently, the struggles over one set of differences are connected with the struggles over another set of differences. Finally, the ensuing tension and its manifestation is an expression of a variety of oppositions. Thus a language riot in Bihar is not necessarily only over language but could perhaps be connected with religion too.

It is this notion of interconnectedness that also makes it possible to establish the relation between television and the existing contradictions in India. For example, the signifying practices of the *Mahabharat* serial are different from the signs and codes used in the regional language broadcasts. Very often these differences are also connected with the ongoing differences between the various social blocs in India. However, by selecting and repeating a particular set of practices over others, a serial such as *Mahabharat* on Doordarshan produces a preferred set of practices as the natural ones in India. The purpose of this work is to examine the signifying strategies that do this, and explore the ways in which many of the contradictions in India are connected to the textual strategies of the *Mahabharat* serial.

The first step is to examine the various contradictions in India. To do this, I shall use four axes of struggle. These represent the centers around which struggle has continued in India. Television has been able to represent, and articulate, its signifying practices with these tensions, producing a set of resolutions as preferred and natural. These struggles are manifest as social and cultural practices articulated with language, regionality, religion and gender. Television, particularly the *Mahabharat* serial, has been able to mobilize

---

[3] Here I use the notion of articulation and ideology as developed by Hall and Laclau within the framework of cultural studies. This, too, has been discussed earlier in Chapter 2.

these elements in its signifying practices, and reproduce a set of preferred ideological positions along these vectors.

However, these directional forces do not work in isolation. Instead, an articulated combination of elements produce the ideological field—the cultural space—where television operates. This is the fundamental point in the theory of articulation: it is within a connection of elements that an articulated sense of culture is produced. I am choosing to highlight these four vectors because they are the ones that, in combination, help to produce a cultural space for India, and are also the ones that are represented on television, and articulated with the signifying practices of television in general, and *Mahabharat* in particular.

The production of cultural space is a key consideration in choosing the vectors. The cultural and signifying practices of Indians are played out in this space. Arguably, there are a large number of vectors to choose from. There are few social and cultural elements in Indian life that do not pose as vectors of contradiction and opposition. The Indian cultural arena can be divided along the lines of caste, class, language, region, religion, gender, age and race, to mention a few. However, within the framework of cultural studies, it is important to be able to focus on those elements that bear a significant impact on the articulated chain that makes up the synthetic network of the cultural map of India. This means that some elements will be highlighted for analysis and explanation, while others will be bracketed within the articulated chain without specific reference to the elements but with an intrinsic recognition of the existence of the conflict, now bound with the four primary vectors that I have chosen to use.

This process first requires a rethinking and elaboration of the elements that are bracketed with the others. Two such vectors are class and caste. Within most sociological study of Indian life, these two appear to be the dominant and primary vectors of analysis. There is always an attempt to reduce class to determining levels of analysis in the reductionist notion of class held by traditional Marxist thinking. Yet European scholars, such as Althusser, argue against this necessary correspondence between class and culture. The entire post-structuralist debate is to examine the determination of culture by class, and to question the linear and unidirectional notion of class base and cultural superstructure. Althusser, Hall and others argue for a Marxism without guarantees where the cultural critic is not ready to accept this necessary correspondence between class and other human activities and practices. Within the theory of articulation, and in a conjunctural view of society, class becomes yet another link in the chain that produces a dominant ideology and a hegemonic order. It is beyond the scope of this work to undertake a detailed discussion of this theoretical position. However, suffice to say that in considering the relation between the text of a television program on Doordarshan and the everyday practices of Indians, the role of class can be bracketed with the contradictions around region, language, religion and gender. In other words, I would argue that class does not play a determining role and its position is overdetermined by a variety of other practices that can be centered around the four critical contradictions just described. However, I would hasten to add that this is not to underestimate the determining effects of class, but to recognize that, in this work, class can be considered to be articulated within the chain created by these four vectors.

In a similar fashion, the notion of caste is also critical in most sociological and religious analyses of Indian life.[4] Caste has often been made the central argument within the study of conflict and contradictions in India, and this has not always been appropriate. Indeed, the notion of caste by itself does not become a particularly powerful force unless it is articulated with other ideological elements (such as religion, ethnicity and economic class). The controversy around the decisions of the Mandal Commission needs to be thought of in terms of a peculiar alignment that was formed between economic opportunity and caste, thus leading to an explosive ideological chain. Yet this alignment was made secondary to the caste view that informed the bloody riots. Sharma (1986) has highlighted this tendency to obtain a 'caste view' of Indian life, attempting to reduce everything to a caste model. This falls into the same trap of reductionism that the class conflict paradigm of Marxism suffered from. Indeed, one key to understanding caste conflict and the contradictions around caste is to recognize the way caste is associated with other contradictions. For instance, Sharma

[4] For a detailed analysis of caste and its relationship with Indian life, the reader can go to a variety of authors (Dumont, 1970; Sherring, 1974; Sharma, 1986). Amongst them, Sharma (1986) forwards an argument about the relationship between caste and class and the way the two can be considered as an articulated whole.

(1986) makes the following point: 'Since caste incorporates class and class incorporates caste, neither "caste view" alone nor "class view" alone would explain the totality of India's social reality'. It is also not difficult to extrapolate this position to India's cultural map, and to incorporate within the regional and linguistic contradictions the issue of caste.

Finally, this work does not analyse India's social reality in toto, but explains, via a television text, the image of India and its cultural map, and the location of television within the map. Therefore, the issues of caste and class need not play a critical determining role but can be bracketed with the other elements. Using the argument proposed by Sharma, it is possible to connect the issues of class and caste and combine them with the four elements that I have used to determine the position of television in the cultural map of India. After this brief digression on two common vectors of contradiction in India, I shall now examine the four elements that will be used in this work.

## The Contradictions

The four elements—language, regionality, religion and gender—are four centers around which discourses have developed in India, and continue to develop. These represent what Grossberg calls the various determinants that, in unity, form the conjunctural view of society in India. As Grossberg has pointed out:

Each form of social practice[5] has its own specificity or 'relative autonomy'; each has its own specific field of effects, particular transformations that it produces and embodies. But the effects of any concrete practice—its conjunctural identity—are always 'overdetermined' by the network of relations in which it is located (Grossberg, 1986).

In this context, I will demonstrate how the struggles around language are closely articulated with the strife between regions of India, as well as with the questions of religion. Religion, on the other hand, is articulated with the struggles around age (particularly in the

[5] in this instance, around language, region, religion, age and gender.

practices that distinguish between the young and the old) and gender, ultimately describing the specific gender roles in India. At the same time, each of these axes divide India in its own specific way, illustrating the relative autonomy of its effects.

Programs on Doordarshan (such as *Mahabharat*) have been appropriating from a number of languages, religions and regions that are contesting with each other for dominance in India. In this process of selective coopting, Doordarshan is redefining what is currently considered the preferred combination of social, religious and cultural elements. However, this is not to suggest that Doordarshan is free of internal inconsistencies. Even as the programs from Delhi, called the National Network programs (as opposed to the regional programs from regional stations), circulate a specific set of linguistic, regional and religious practices, the local stations contest them. At this point, it will be useful to examine the various axes of struggle, and the way television is specifically positioned among these differences in India.

## Language

India has never been able to claim any unity of language. The preferred language of India, if indeed one exists or can be found, has constantly been contested. The diversity is expressed in the variety of different scripts and spoken dialects that are used in India. However, from this diversity, through a process of historical selection, Hindi has been chosen as the preferred language in India. Over the past two decades, Indian television has also facilitated this process.

Historically, Sanskrit is considered to be the earliest Indian language. The principal religious and historical texts in India have been written in Sanskrit, for example, the Mahabharat epic is described as the longest Indian epic, composed of thousands of Sanskrit couplets. It is the language associated with Hindu religion and Hindu religious books, (such as the Vedas and Upanishads), which were composed originally in Sanskrit and then translated into other Indian languages. Consequently, Sanskrit is also articulated with the Hindu religion.[6] The present form of Hindi is an

---

[6] This is pointed out in the work of Kinsley (1982) who justifies the claim that the language of Hinduism and its proponent was indeed Sanskrit.

offshoot of Sanskrit and it is, therefore, able to establish a certain binding with the Hindu religion as well.

The tensions around language, however, began with the arrival of the powerful Persian invaders who brought with them the tradition of the Arabic language and script. This was the language of the Islamic tradition, with its connection with Islam, the *Koran*, and the Islamic rulers who invaded India and posed a threat to Hinduism. Thus the opposition between the languages became associated with the disparity between religions.[7]

The Islamic 'invaders'[8] also occupied parts of India. In those regions, Islamic languages dominated, removing Sanskrit from its position of importance. Thus regions get imaged around languages, precisely in the way Benedict Anderson (1983) has imagined nations around languages. The combination of the three is expressed by King, who says: 'dozens of different languages are spoken in India, each by millions of people, each having extraordinarily powerful claims on ethnic, regional, religious and ancestral loyalties' (King, 1986). Language, therefore, becomes a discourse around which tensions develop and get articulated with the contradictions around region and religion.

Within an atmosphere of self-determination following independence, the language issue became even more critical. There have been countless 'language riots' where the key issue has been the dominance of one language over another. The conflict is around the question of Hindi: most struggles are around the imposition of Hindi as a common Indian language, particularly in regions that have historically not been articulated with Hindi. This is especially true of southern and eastern India, where there is a popular disapproval of Hindi, which has been manifested in language riots.

Riots like these also question the notion of Hindi as the national

---

[7] This issue is pointed out by Weiner who says,

Urdu speakers, for example, have called for the establishment of Urdu as an official second language of the states in which they live. There are large Urdu-speaking communities in Uttar Pradesh, Bihar, Maharashtra, Andhra and Karnataka; in these states, an overwhelming majority of Muslims report Urdu as their mother-tongue (Weiner, 1986).

[8] There is an intrinsic marginalization in the use of the word 'invaders'. However, the point remains that Islamic arrival was from outside India and so, in popular culture, it has been constructed as the 'invaders'.

language. Since independence, this has become an ongoing area of debate. This tension was first manifest when it was proposed that Hindi, and not Hindustani,[9] would be the national language, and English would be phased out. This is the point when the Hindi-speaking hegemony began to win its position of leadership by reproducing the language closely associated with Sanskrit and Hinduism as the official national language of the nation.

In the past few years, *Mahabharat* on Doordarshan has also been able to reproduce Hindi as the language of *bharat*, emphasizing that Hindi is indeed the language in which the greatest epics of India are read and produced. *Mahabharat* on television has been circulated using a Hindi dialect that is archetypical of north-central India. This Hindi differs from what is spoken in Bombay, Calcutta and other parts of India where Hindi has been replanted. The use of a specific type of Hindi only emphasizes the point that pure Hindi is the language that is representative of a small section of India, and corrupt forms are used elsewhere. The articulation between Hindi and classical Indian literature is established by using pure Hindi which has not been corrupted by other languages such as Urdu and Panjabi. This contrast becomes most apparent when the *Mahabharat* serial is compared with the serial *The Sword of Tipu Sultan*, which uses a different kind of Hindi—one with strong overtones of Urdu—thus emphasizing the difference between the Hindi of the north Indian Hindus and the Hindi of the Deccan Plateau where the influence of Islam was more pronounced.[10]

The contradictions around Hindi as a synthesized language are highlighted by Dimock et al. (1974). They point out that Hindi is a range of languages. It has been influenced by the works of the

[9] This is a synthetic language that was proposed by Mahatma Gandhi, who was conscious of the contradictions around language in India. Weiner (1986) describes the fate of Hindustani: 'Gandhi's advocacy of a slightly factitious official 'Hindustani,' neutral between Hindi and Urdu, was less an advocacy of something linguistically real than a well-meant effort to preserve communal peace'. Hindustani was not adopted because it was defeated in Parliament when the question of adopting an official language came up in 1946.

[10] From the beginning, there was a certain amount of doubt about the success of this serial, simply because it focused on an Islamic hero, as compared to the staple of Hindu heros. This doubt is expressed by Shobha Sengupta in saying, 'the controversial' *Sword of Tipu Sultan* has begun at last. The first few episodes have impressed and, if true worth is to be victorious, Inshallah, all of this serial will be telecast' (*The Telegraph*, June 1990).

Persian poet Amir Khusrau as well as Hindu Poets such as Tulsidas, whose most notable work is the Hindi version of the *Ramayan* story. Notably, on Doordarshan, this version provided the framework of the television script.

In spite of the ways in which Hindi and other languages have merged with each other, the articulation between Hindi and Sanskrit is perhaps the most pronounced. As Dimock points out: 'The regional literatures frequently borrowed forms from Sanskrit: *The Ramayan* of Valmiki appears in the sixteenth-century Hindi of Tulsidas' (Dimock, et al., 1974). Hindi, therefore, is not free of internal inconsistencies and Doordarshan, by appropriating north Indian Hindi, has been able to circulate this particular form of the language as the preferred language of *Mahabharat*. However, this is true not only of the *Mahabharat* serial. *Ramayan*, which was telecast earlier, also used the same form of Hindi. Also, a majority of the programs distributed by the National Network of Delhi are in Hindi. These compete with telecasts from the regional centers, which use the regional languages. This highlights the tension between the language of a particular region and the language that is preferred by the central broadcast system in Delhi. This tension came to a head when the local stations were directed to abandon their regional language news programs and carry only the central news telecast from Delhi.

In short, Doordarshan, in its National Network, has constantly used Hindi as the central language of India. Through serials such as *Mahabharat* and *Buniyaad*, and amongst countless other genres of programs, Doordarshan has been able to project Hindi as the preferred language of the medium. Earlier, serials such as *Buniyaad* and *Hum Log*, and other Delhi based programs on the National Network, were mostly in Hindi too. Moreover, the existing difference between regions is reproduced in the selective use of language on television. This has resulted in the marginalization of other official and unofficial languages in India. However, some of the differences have been resolved by the inclusion of infrequent programs in other languages (such as regional language feature films and music and dance programs) bringing other languages back into the mainstream. But, by calling them 'regional language feature film' and 'serial in Hindi', the opposition between the languages is reiterated.

Moreover, Hindi has been the language of the burgeoning feature film industry of India. In the popular culture of India, Hindi cinema plays a crucial role, and the very name—Hindi cinema— places this cultural formation in a particular linguistic position. This is an articulation between television and cinema in India that has only been able to emphasize the linguistic alliance of Doordarshan. It is, therefore, possible to claim that television in India, and particularly serials like *Mahabharat*, have reproduced an ideological field where the articulation between the medium and Hindi has been dominant and preferred.

This struggle is also articulated with the question of regionality. Hindi was not only bound to Hindu tradition but was also the language of the northern Indian states, and was thus in opposition to the languages of the south Indian states which had their own script and language. This led to violent struggles in Madras, a city in south India, in 1965—twenty years after independence.

## Regionality

Every region in India claims a specific set of everyday material activities specific to the region. These activities include language, religious rituals and cultural preferences. For example, the celebration of the defeat of Ravana at the hands of Ram is reproduced through different cultural and religious rituals in different parts of India. Although this event remains a key religious event in the Hindu tradition, in northern India the celebrations are different from eastern India, which are different from southern India.

In addition to the differences in religious practices, regions in India are also split by linguistic, social and cultural practices. Almost every region in India has a distinct language. Social and cultural practices also remain distinct within regions. For example, the cultural formations around music and dance become specific to locale—the nomadic bands of West Bengal in eastern India have a unique musical style which is different from the musical practices of the north Indian gypsies.[11] These practices are in a struggle for dominance in imaging a sense of regionality, and also in circulating which practices would be produced as the preferred and dominant ones in the larger sense of the Indian nation.

[11] This is a reference to the *bauls*, a roving group of singers in Bengal who, in their ballads and songs, celebrate the romantic love between Krishna and his consort Radha.

The question of regionality is thus contested at two levels. First, in describing what practices within specific regions will be preferred.[12] Secondly, regions are contesting at the national level to produce the practices of particular regions as the preferred national ones.[13]

Finally, these issues converge in political tension when particular regions demand autonomy from the Union, attempting to redefine a geographic space not as a dominant region but as a separate state altogether. The secessionist movements in Kashmir, Assam and Punjab are illustrative of this struggle. The question of regional divergence is, therefore, acute and its resolution will ultimately describe what emerges as an Indian nation. This crisis is highlighted by Madhok: 'They [the social bloc that demands separate nationhood for separate regions] expect people living in those states, including minority groups, to become good Maharastrians. Tamils or Gujaratis rather than good Indians' (Madhok, 1970). Such regional struggles, concentrated around the question of language for instance, are common to this part of the globe. The country of Bangladesh emerged from such a struggle when East Pakistan opposed the Urdu hegemony of West Pakistan. The current violence in Sri Lanka is also centered around a region that speaks Tamil. The contradictions over regions, therefore, are vital in the ideological field in this part of the world.

These are the differences that are reproduced on Doordarshan too. The *Mahabharat* serial has been shot entirely in the tradition of the north Indian rendering of the text. Although the same text has been translated and illustrated in various other Indian languages, it was the dominant north Indian Hindi and Sanskrit centric version that was appropriated for television. This is illustrated in the visual images that have been used in *Mahabharat*. The set design, clothes and surrounding, all reproduce the illustrations drawn from the north Indian Hindi renderings of the text.[14] The palaces, garments and the lush Gangetic Plains of central and north India are meticulously reproduced in the visual images in the

---

[12] In Bihar, for instance, the clashes over Urdu and Hindi represent this aspect of the struggle.

[13] The production of a specific dance form as *bharatnatyam*, or the archetypical Indian dance, represents this aspect of the struggle.

[14] It is important to point out that this is already produced in the popular culture as the dominant interpretation of the visual images of the Mahabharat by other texts, such as comic books, illustrations and the film *Mahabharat*.

serial. The same holds true for *Ramayan*. These signifying practices reproduce the regional differences, ultimately marginalizing the other versions of the epic. For example, the Bengali literary version of the epic is different in its reproduction of the narrative, and in the description of the setting and clothes. If this version had been used for the television serial, *Mahabharat* on Doordarshan would perhaps have turned out quite differently. However, other versions were marginalized by adopting the Hindi version and circulating the version of the Mahabharat which is closest to the north central Indian tradition.

Most of National Network is similar to *Mahabharat* in this sense. Other programs, ranging from serials such as *Buniyaad* and *Hum log* to tele-plays, also represent north India as the location for the tales. For example, in a serialized program called *Chote Babu* which recounted the challenges of middle class life, the city was an unnamed small town in north India where everybody spoke Hindi. Many other examples of television programs can be used to illustrate a process where the surroundings, rituals and activities of the people constantly place them, and the events, in a specific part of India. For instance, when the grandmother in one of the family melodramas on National Network is called *dadi*, and she wears her sari in a fashion peculiar to older women in north and central India, she becomes distinct from the image of a grandmother from West Bengal who might appear in a Bengali serial from Calcutta. In its variety of genres, Doordarshan is able to repetitively use signs that distinguish between regions, with the National Network from Delhi steadfastly reproducing the north Indian set of images.

A good example is drawn from the genre of sports programs. The dichotomy between regional sports programs and the programs on National Network does not only set up a difference between the centers of distribution but also in the articulation of a region with specific linguistic and sporting practices. An example of this is available in the sports programs broadcast from Calcutta, as opposed to those broadcast from Delhi. Typically, the Delhi programs are broadcast in Hindi while the Calcutta programs are in Bengali. In addition, while the National broadcast covers a wide variety of sports, the local program concentrates on sporting activities in Calcutta and Bengal. This is mainly, football. Football has been historically articulated with Bengal. In the popular culture of Bengal, football has been considered the archetypical Bengali sport. In fact, there are numerous references to football in the popular culture of Bengal, from the movie *Football* to music that refers to this sport. This articulation is reproduced on the local broadcasts too. Any football game in Calcutta is carried by the station for local broadcast. The commentary is in Bengali, and is in contrast with the Hindi commentary of other sports that are telecast on the National Network. Only when football is played with teams appearing from states other than Bengal is the game telecast on the National Network with a Hindi commentary.

This signifying process only reproduces the contradictory relationship between the states and the center, where some states are marginalized to maintain the dominance of the Center and its allies. This only emphasizes the differences between regions, projecting a particular region, and the practices of that region, as preferred while others are sidelined as typically 'regional'.

Moreover, the discourse around region is also condensed with the discourses around language. By binding Hindi and north India as the central locus of practices, *Mahabharat* and other north Indian Hindi serials are able to marginalize the possibility of non-Hindi serials coming out of this center. Indeed, the unity of Hindi and north Indian discourse leads to the marginalization of the discourses that are grouped around other languages (such as Assamese, from the eastern state of Assam). By constantly reproducing the hegemony of the north Indian Hindi belt, National Network on Doordarshan has been able to largely ignore the practices that are related to other languages and other parts of India. The occasional film in a regional language, and perhaps some region-specific programs, are mostly what come out of Delhi's National Network. In the end, it is a north Indian hegemony that is being perpetuated, which is in total alignment with what is circulated in the *Mahabharat* tale. This is pointed out by Kinsley: 'The historical setting [of the Mahabharat] is one in which rulers of settled peoples compete with each other for control of the North Indian plains' (Kinsley, 1982).

Moreover, the issue of religion becomes articulated with regionality and geographic space. For example, the struggle for a Sikh homeland in Punjab is closely bound to the fact that there is indeed a large section of the country which claims a vast Sikh population. Similarly, the geographic proximity of West Bengal with Bangladesh makes West Bengal a region that has a high concentration of Muslims. Also, those parts of India that were under Islamic rule (for instance, the region of the Deccan Plateau in southern India) have a greater Islamic tradition than other parts of India.

## Religions

Among the non-Hindu blocs, the largest, of course, are the Indian Muslims.[15] The tension between the Hindus and Muslims is evident in a variety of *material activities* in contemporary India i.e., everyday practices of the people which make up the everyday lived experiences and actions of a social group. This is illustrated by inflammable comments by the nation's politicians, one of whom has said:

> we are conscious that not merely getting into power, or acquiring representation in Parliament and in legislatures, should be our concern. We are also interested in projecting the nationalistic viewpoint we represent and the commitment that this is our ancient nation . . . whose culture is essentially Hindu' (from the text of the speech delivered by the Bharatiya Janata Party president, L.K. Advani, to a gathering in Coimbatore published in *The Telegraph*, 17 May 1990).

However, the reply to this speech by a leading Muslim intellectual represents the complexity of the relationships between religion and other elements in popular cultural space. In 'A Muslim's Response to L.K. Advani,' published in the same newspaper, Saeed Naqvi writes:

> No, Mr. Advani, you are wrong . . . . Ram, Krishna and all the elements of our great mythology have been part of our culture, our songs, poetry, literature . . . if by some magic I could have some say, I would have had Sanskrit as our national language. Everyone of us, from Kanyakumari to Kashmir, would have had to put in equal effort to learn the language which is the basis of our common culture (Naqvi, *The Telegraph*, 26 May 1990).

[15] Weiner reports that in the 1981 census, Muslims constituted 11.4 per cent of the Indian population representing nearly seventy-six million people.

Needless to say, there is a whole range of complex elements linked together, with a Muslim willing to accept Sanskrit as a national language when Sanskrit is the traditional Hindu language, and with a Muslim claiming that Hindu incarnations such as Ram and Krishna are a part of the Indian nation and culture. I shall end this argument with one last quote from one of the numerous letters to the editor following Advani's speech and Naqvi's response:

> In his article, Mr Naqvi insists that Muslims have made great contributions to Indian culture. True, and so have Christians, Buddhists and Sikhs. But Muslims living in India should identify themselves wholly as Indians. When India loses a cricket match against Pakistan, the joy in some Muslim pockets is quite apparent (Subhro Mazumdar, letter to the editor, *The Telegraph*, 9 June 1990).

These excerpts illustrate the complexity of the contradictions around the question of religion and how, indeed, it is articulated with a variety of other practices that are common in India's popular culture. The last quote, in fact, establishes an articulation between sport, religion and region by collating religious ideology with a region and with a particular sporting practice.

*Mahabharat* and *Ramayan* on Doordarshan have also been reproducing a Hindu hegemony by circulating two epics that are typically connected with Hindu ideology and Hindu practices. The articulation between the epics, and Hinduism, is widely recognized, as pointed out by Kinsley, who describes the texts as the two pillars of Hindu literature. This is emphasized by the variety of Hindu religious rituals that are shown in the serial. For example, a set of episodes focus on the *Rajasuya* ceremony of Yudhistir, when he is crowned the monarch of Indraprastha. Kinsley describes this ceremony saying: 'The *rajasuya* ceremony is illustrative of Vedic ritual as a whole. The many rituals that make up the *rajasuya* are often variations of shorter Vedic rituals; the themes that dominate the ceremony are typically Vedic' (Kinsley, 1982).[16] It is these rituals that are meticulously reproduced in the broadcast too. This, and other such textual strategies, establish the discursive

---

[16] The same author reminds that the Vedas are the central religious doctrines of Hindu theology, comparable to the Christian Old Testament.

connection between *Mahabharat* and *Ramayan* on Doordarshan and Hindu hegemony.

The repetitive portrayal of Hindu customs in the *Mahabharat* serial also needs to be connected with the growth of Hindu fundamentalism in India, spearheaded by the Vishva Hindu Parishad (VHP), (the Indian Hindu League). The practices of religion have been articulated with political practices, and the currently popular VHP leaders have been able to mobilize popular Hindu feeling, best embodied in the following quote:

> This [the upsurge of violence in Ayodhya, and the politicization of religion] is the result of the lopsided attitude of the politicians. The Hindus have always received stepmotherly treatment from them and are now rebelling against politicians (Neeraja Shukla, quoted by Badhwar in *India Today*, 1991).

This lack is fulfilled by serials such as *Mahabharat*, where Hindus can find the long sought Hindu center. Here the centrality of television, and the Mahabharat epic, come together to produce a public forum where Hinduism is rediscovered, for instance, in the star who plays Krishna, or the sets that recreate Hastinapur. Ultimately, it is the physical existence of the wood and glass television set that brings the Gods home.[17] It is thus no surprise that the actors in *Mahabharat* are raised to the stature of Gods, and the television set becomes a locus of worship. To emphasize this, I shall return to the example of the actor who plays the part of Arjun: in order to hide his Muslim identity, he changed his stage name to 'Arjun', collapsing his textual identity with his extra-textual identity. This only illustrates that within Hindu hegemony, the possibility of a Muslim playing the role of a Pandava is non-existent, unnatural and deviant.

## Gender and Age

Superimposed and articulated with these contradictions now arise questions around gender. The position of women within Hinduism

[17] This needs to be related with the *puja* space in most Hindu homes. This is a space that is set aside, either an entire room or part of a room, where religious idols are kept, and typically the women of the household worship these idols on a daily basis. Similarly, in many homes, when *Mahabharat* or *Ramayan* would be telecast, the television set would become the *puja* space in the home.

(and Islam) has always been secondary to that of men. In the overembracing patriarchy of Hinduism (and Islam), the woman has been produced as dominated and marginalized. This has been possible by the articulation of a variety of social and cultural practices that place the man in a position of dominance. For example, within the Hindu tradition, the practice of *sati* (where a widow was burnt alive on the funeral pyre of her dead husband) became a representation of the relative position of the sexes in the structure of Hindu society. Such practices have been able to set up a male hegemony and, within this ideological field, the social location of an individual becomes described by one's sex.

The perpetuation of this male hegemony is evident in the practices that are still followed in some parts of India, specially in north-central India. A shocking example of this is the recent report of a *sati* which was performed in Rajasthan, a part of the Hindi speaking Hindu belt. In the October 1987 issue of *India Today*, a 'pagan sacrifice' was reported in a village of Rajasthan. The journal goes on to say: 'The incident, with the massive social acceptance, even approbation, it has received, would probably not have attracted much national attention were it not for the sustained opposition of women's groups in the state' (Staff, *India Today*, October 1987). This demonstrates two issues:, the perpetuation of a male Hindu hegemony that was able to perform this ghastly practice in the late eighties, as well as the existence of the struggle against such a hegemony.

This is, therefore, not an uncontested position. Particularly in post-colonial India, the question of gender has been the focus of struggle though perhaps not in the same terms of feminist movements in the industrialized West, but in redefining the location of the sexes in a social societal hierarchy.[18] This has been possible by the growth of women's movements and by questioning the hegemonic leadership of the male. The social position of women has been the result of a variety of social modes of action, religious

---

[18] As Bumiller's (1990) book illustrates, women's struggles in India cannot necessarily be captured within the framework of a Western sense of 'feminist' movements. The tensions around gender in India have to be understood in political, social, cultural and religious action to oppose a variety of interconnected oppressions. Every chapter in Bumiller's book, *May you be the Mother of a Hundred Sons*, deals with different oppressions and offers examples of how women in India have been able to overcome them.

rituals, and political action that range from *sati* to the exchange of dowry. Changes are manifest in the way that this disempowered group is now finding a voice through organized bodies, as pointed out by Minault:

> I see women's advocacy of women's rights becoming a more vibrant force in Indian society, and find an increasing tendency for women, regardless of class, to confront patriarchal authority, whether landlords, the police or exploitative employers. Young women are also challenging the traditional power of the their mothers-in-law (Minault, 1986).

What Minault points out is the struggle that is visible in India now in disarticulating the traditional position of women, and rearticulating gender with a position of power. However, this is not a conflict that works in isolation. The practices that have shaped the gender roles in India are also articulated with the questions around religion. It is, therefore, not enough to challenge just mothers-in-law or landlords but to question the entire ideological field that is produced around these several forces.

In the same vein, *Mahabharat* on Doordarshan reproduces the gendered practices that are specific to a Hindu-Hindi-north Indian tradition. This is done through a variety of narrative and textual practices. First, the wife is almost always 'won' after a tournament where the various men participate in a competitive sport, perhaps archery, and win the woman. Secondly, as in the case of Draupadi, the wife is constructed as a person who is not only inserted within patriarchal hegemony, but within a system of family where the mother-in-law is produced as the center of female power. Thus, when the mother of the Pandavas, unknowingly, asks the five brothers to share the 'prize' that Arjun had won, there is no option but to accept Draupadi as the wife of all the five brothers. This reestablishes the hegemony of the mother/mother-in-law in a social location. Indeed, Krishna endorse this, and points out that once a mother has said something, the sons have no option but to carry out her orders. This emphasizes the Hindu mother-son/mother-in-law-daughter-in-law articulations. The possibility of questioning the mother/mother-in-law is marginalized, indeed that possibility is made non-existent and deviant, particularly by the intervention of Krishna. Such practices constantly replace the woman in a very well defined and uncontested position within the structure of the text and, metonymically, the structure of society.

A third signifying practice that reinserts the woman in the patri-archal system is the role that is reproduced for the woman in the text. 'She' is the procreator.[19] Across the entire narrative, the woman is the 'mother' who gives birth to upholders of either *dharma* or *adharma*. And it is in her role as the procreator that she becomes powerful. This is the only practice that gives her any power in the narrative and, as if to bring her back within male hegemony, even this power becomes open to male dominance. The story of the birth of Dhritarashtra is illustrative of this argu-ment. Dhritarashtra was born blind because his mother, on seeing the dishevelled ascetic who would be Dhritarashtra's father, closed her eyes, resulting in a curse from the ascetic, who ordained that her son would be born blind. This only reproduces the relative position of the man in controlling the practices of the other sex.

Doordarshan also uses similar sets of representations for women across a large array of programs, from serials such as *Buniyaad* to *Chehere*. The same north Indian style of wearing a sari, with the typical cover for the head, the dot on the forehead and the infre-quent use of Western-style clothes for the middle class Indian woman all draw a thread of semiotic similarity on television, reproducing and recirculating a specific image of the Indian woman on television.[20]

However, a contradiction is set up between the serial *Mahabharat* and the other texts on television, particularly the genres of talk shows and programs for women. Shows such as *Ghare Baire*, question the very practices that are reproduced on *Mahabharat*. However, by articulating feminine practices with the story of *bharat* and Hinduism, *Mahabharat* is able to circulate a much more ideologically preferred gender position than talk shows can achieve. This contradictory relationship is indeed the site of struggle but

[19] There is also the predominant image of the Mother Goddess in Hindu practices. Durga is the archetypical Mother Goddess whom Ram worships before setting out on his crusade against the evil Ravan in *Ramayan*. Thus, the mother as the Mother Goddess is a central image in Hindu practices too.

[20] Interestingly, the female newscasters on television news are most often clad in saris, that being preferred as the female attire in India. The specificity of television is here in the non-coercive way in which a particular dress is popularized, as compared to the oppressive ways in which women are made to wear *chaddars* in Iran.

there seems to be little questioning of the hegemony produced by the articulation of religion, language and gender.

Women's shows have not been able to mobilize or question that articulation. Just by examining the position of women little can be achieved until the entire ideological field is addressed and questioned. The problem lies precisely here—a text like the Mahabharat is sacrosanct because it is the story of _bharat_, and to question that would be to question all that is archetypical Indian. Thus the oppression of women in the Mahabharat becomes an insignificant element in the articulated unity of the Mahabharat.

The ideological field around gender is thus centered around Hindu ideology, and bound with the practices of north India and Hindi. The possibility of questioning this is left closed in the _Mahabharat_ serial. This is then articulated with the social and cultural practices that describe the gender position, which is the product of these complex chains, particularly those grouped around religion. The archetypical mother—a key role in Hindu ideology—is reproduced, and the woman is reinserted within a patriarchal hegemony. In reproducing this as natural and preferred, the voices of opposition, particularly of those who would reexamine the position of the woman, are marginalized and produced as deviant.

In India, the notion of age represents another similar vector. For example, in the _Mahabharat_ serial the difference between the old and young is signified in the form of address, where the old is addressed in a specific way by the young, and the elders in the narrative address the younger, positioning them in a specific place within the hierarchy of age, and simultaneously reproducing the dominance of the elders.

This dominance is best illustrated in a situation where it is challenged—in the episode where the hierarchy of age is overridden by a different hierarchy, that of divinity. When Krishna approaches the grandfather of the Pandavas, Krishna solicits the elder's blessing by touching the elder's feet. However, Bhisma, the grandfather, reminds Krishna that Krishna's divine position makes him superior to Bhisma, in spite of the fact that Krishna is younger in age. Age and divinity are set up in opposition here, and what is circulated is that age is indeed secondary to divinity, and the incarnation of Gods is, above all, independent of age.[21]

---

[21] It is thus no surprise that in early 1991 a young girl became the object of worship in Orissa when she miraculously started healing people—thus being produced as divine incarnation.

In some episodes Krishna offers a blessing, and the camera closes up on him, keeping the receiver of the blessing out of the frame, collapsing the textual receiver of the blessing with the viewer at home. This is precisely how Krishna is brought home, as a living being, offering his blessing to all who are watching the serial. This purposive collapsing of the textual addressee and the implied addressee (that is, the viewer) is what Stam (1983) has called the 'regime of the fictive We'. Here it is no longer Arjun or Yudhistir who is the recipient of the blessing, but the people watching Krishna, who 'hails' them into the subject position in Hindu ideology.[22]

Finally this Hindu, Hindi, patriarchal hegemony of north India is articulated with the fundamental struggle in the Mahabharat—the struggle between *dharma* and *adharma*. Across the entire serial, in every episode, this struggle has been reproduced. In the opening sequence, the musical score emphasizes the story of the Mahabharat as the story of struggle between good and evil, and the ultimate resolution of the struggle is embodied in the reestablishment of the rule of *dharma*. All that opposes *dharma* is deviant and will finally be destroyed.

This rule of *dharma* is then bound to the social and cultural practices of the Pandavas, whose practices only reproduce the social, cultural and religious practice of the Hindu-Hindi-male hegemony. By mobilizing this articulation between *dharma* and the hegemony of this social bloc, any possibilities of opposition are marginalized. Indeed, in the text, whoever questions this hegemony is dealt with violently, and the rule of the Pandavas, and consequently the rule of *dharma*, prevails.

In the closing section of each episode, the viewer is reminded that the story of the Mahabharat is the story of *bharat* where the righteous have been able to challenge evil and win the struggle for hegemony. The articulation between *bharat* and India naturalizes the ideological field that is produced around the discourse of *dharma*, the Pandavas, Krishna and a sense of India as Hindu country. Here, again, any possibility of opposition is excluded.

[22] The question of 'hailing' is connected with the Althusserian notion of interpellation, where by the work of ideology, in this instance the 'regime of the fictive We,' the viewer is interpellated into a subject position in and of ideology (Hall, 1980b).

## In Summary

Some conclusions need to be drawn from this discussion on contradictions. Based on Hall's views, it is possible to argue that social relations and locations are generated as a product of the articulation of a set of contradictory elements. These social relations and locations tend to be 'over-determined', the positions being produced by a unity of contradictory determinants. Fundamentally, the unity that is produced remains non-necessary and open to ideological struggle and questioning.

Hall explains ideological struggle as the process by which a particular ideological chain and the unity it produces becomes the site of struggle and, in the end, it is ruptured to produce a new set of articulations. This unity is thus not a seamless and necessary one but the product of a process, where the forces of domination have been able to produce certain articulations as dominant. To some extent, this is the result of a residual set of practices that have been perpetuated by the hegemonic leadership of a dominant social bloc. King suggests this in saying:

> The framers of the Constitution of India accorded constitutional standing to most of the major regional languages of India and to Sanskrit, but they chose Hindi, the regional language with the most speakers and the heaviest political clout, as the official language of the union (King, 1986).

This is an example where ideological struggle is reproduced as a struggle over practices, where the practice of using Hindi as the preferred language becomes dominant.

The unified social location is also described by a set of material activities that the members of a social position perform. This is the Althusserian notion of ideology, where ideology becomes a set of material everyday practices. Thus the articulated elements that produce popular culture only reproduce the set of conventions that are articulated with the struggles over language, region, religion and gender. Ideology operates through the various practices that, in combination, over-determine the social location of a bloc of people. Thus the fused location of a Hindu woman of north India is the product of an articulation of the practices of performing a daily worship of Ram and Krishna, speaking Hindi, bringing a television set as dowry at the time of marriage and watching *Mahabharat* on it. It is such an articulation of practices that has become dominant and circulated and it is these practices that need to be questioned and fought against.

Just as the elements that produce unity struggle with each other, these congealed positions themselves are in a state of struggle with each other, each trying to emerge as the dominant ideological field in India. In this struggle over hegemonic leadership, certain combinations of elements are being produced and reproduced as preferred and dominant, as illustrated in the adoption of Hindi as the official language of the country.

Ultimately, discourses that challenge the hegemony of the current leadership—be it religious, economic or political—are reproduced within popular culture as deviant and non-national, where the 'national' itself remains a site of struggle. For example, by representing the disturbances in Kashmir as the 'work of terrorists'[23] a number of questions are marginalized. These are questions that are related with the geographic location of Kashmir, its religious structures and its struggle with the Hindu hegemony of the center in New Delhi. Weiner points out that 'Muslims are India's largest minority, but in Jammu and Kashmir it is the Hindus who regard themselves as the minority' (Weiner, 1986). This is symbolically resolved by reproducing the Muslim struggles in Kashmir as the isolated work of terrorists supported by Pakistan. This was illustrated in a news program on Doordarshan called *Focus* which addressed the Kashmir issue:

Nalini Singh has made a propaganda program for the government of India. No holds barred, no punches pulled and subtlety was thrown out of the window. The Indian case was put through with admirable thoroughness (Shobha Sengupta, *The Telegraph*, 9 June 1990).

This also illustrates that the chain of equivalences that produce the image of 'Kashmir terrorists' is in conflict with the discourses produced around the arguments presented by Sengupta.

[23] This represents a naturalized condensed position that smoothes out an array of contradictory elements by articulating them together into the image of 'terrorists'.

Finally, there is an ongoing crisis of hegemony, where the leadership of a particular social bloc is never guaranteed. Indeed, this is a fundamental assumption within Gramsci's notion of hegemony—that it is an ongoing struggle to gain a position of leadership, albeit not through coercive means.

The crisis of leadership in India has been felt at many points in history, particularly in terms of the social-political bloc that has been able to control the central government in New Delhi.[24] This is precisely where the question of television becomes crucial, since it offers a controlled site where this hegemonic struggle can be contested. The medium becomes the site where these various discourses are articulated together, and are circulated within the popular culture.

This earlier analysis indicates that there is, indeed, a specific hegemony that is being circulated on Doordarshan. This circulation has been possible by the specific use of television's signifying practices in a variety of programs on Doordarshan. This work establishes the precise conclusion that the hegemony of the Hindu-Hindi belt is being perpetuated by serials like *Mahabharat* and *Ramayan* and, in the popular culture, the voices of the marginalized are getting increasingly smothered. This is precisely why a serial such as *The Sword of Tipu Sultan* is prey to controversy and elimination from the flow of Doordarshan. The recognition of this hegemony indeed opens up questions about what is being constructed as oppositional, and for what purpose.[25]

This discussion also begs the question of the 'nation'. The ideological field that is being produced is ultimately reshaping the image of India itself. It is within these articulated practices that an image of national popular culture emerges. By preferring one set of practices over others, and marginalizing one set of practices,

[24] At every instant of crisis, the television medium has been mobilized too. Indira mobilized Doordarshan to justify the need for Emergency. This was achieved particularly through the censoring of news of political and social struggles that would question her hegemony. Later, the struggle over Hindu hegemony continued at a time when 93 per cent of the country was watching *Mahabharat* or *Ramayan* on television.

[25] In other words, this suggests that television is not without its internal contradictions. The selective tradition of television prioritized a combination of elements in popular culture. Yet, as the final chapter in this work will demonstrate, Doordarshan has a large variety of other programs that question the ideological field that is produced by the National Network programs such as *Mahabharat*.

television is able to reproduce a national image that is built around the ideological field described here—this is precisely the role television can, and does, play in India's popular culture. Within this 'nation', a systematic process is eliminating a set of paradigmatic choices, and reproducing a hegemony of the preferred and powerful social bloc.

This is the focus of the next chapter, where the conclusions drawn here are used to rethink the image of the Indian nation produced by *Mahabharat* and by television.

# 6

# Television and the Nation: Doordarshan's India

*India is a volatile mix of religious and ethnic groups
. . . each community with their own, and often
conflicting, demands.*

**Mike Chinnoy,** *reporting from New Delhi for CNN
Special Report following the assassination of
Rajiv Gandhi on 21 May 1991.*

**Mike Chinnoy, in his report**, is reemphasizing the various contradictions in India. From this 'volatile mix', Doordarshan selects a small set of interconnected elements for representation on television. This, in turn, produces a national image of India on Doordarshan. The question that becomes important is the way in which Doordarshan is able to reproduce a particular national image, which is composed of a set of practices, that is circulated as national in India[1]. Consequently, the next question concerns the ideologically preferred image of nation that is being produced and circulated within popular culture.[2]

---

[1] The term 'practice' is being used in the same sense as explained in the earlier chapter—as a set of material activities.

[2] The concept of the 'nation' is itself a contested one, and a variety of approaches can be used to think of the nation. These vary from the historical perspective of Deutsch and others, to the Gramscian notion of civil society as well as Anderson's imagined communities.

A variety of interrelated approaches can be used to understand India as a nation. A framework for conceptualizing a nation can be constructed from the various ways in which the 'nation' has been understood. The nation is, first, a historically produced entity, born out of struggle and ridden with internal contradictions and differences[3]. These struggles and contradictions are played out between the diverse social formations that make up the nation. This is precisely what India faced in the early days following independence. As Rajiv Gandhi pointed out when describing the post-independence challenges of India:

> when we look at a country which is the size of India . . . in area roughly the size of Europe . . . more diverse than Europe, more languages, more ethnically diverse, more regions, nobody believed India would remain united into one (Rajiv Gandhi in the documentary *Life and Death of a Dynasty*).

Yet, India did emerge as a 'nation' not without its contradiction and struggles, but as an unified entity that is still struggling to find a dominant national image.

The struggles are fought using different apparatuses of hegemony, through which the dominant social formations contest and then circulate a specific image of the nation.[4] This image is produced around a set of unique material activities, geographic spaces and social and cultural conventions which are struggling with each other for dominance.[5] In India this struggle is played out on Doordarshan.

---

[3] A variety of traditions are used in coming to these conclusions. There is a range of work (Deutsch and Foltz, 1966; Lerner, 1958; Shafer, 1955; Davis 1978; Amin, 1980) which has focused on the step-wise emergence of nations through various historic events.

[4] Here the work of Gramsci on the state and civil society become pivotal. Readers of Gramsci, such as Carnoy (1984), argue that Gramsci conceptualizes the state, or the nation, as the sum of civil and political society. In the former, various non-coercive instruments of hegemony operate to perpetuate the leadership of a specific social bloc. This is also where Althusser's notion of ideology and its operation through ideological state apparatuses, become generative in regard to a dominant imaging of the nation.

[5] The notion of 'imaging' or 'imagining' a nation is derived from the works of Anderson (1983), who argues for imaging a nation around a set of practices, for instance those of language.

Doordarshan is able to redefine India, and determine what becomes the nationally preferred Indian image. This definition of India is composed of a variety of contradictory multidirectional drives that are precariously held together, or articulated, at any moment in history. Moreover, this articulation is struggled over, and new articulations are constantly produced. India, in fact, emerges as the articulated unity of a variety of practices that revolve around the centers of language, region, religion, and so on.

Doordarshan reproduces a selective set of languages, religions and regions in attempting to produce an unequivocal, homogeneous national image. This is achieved by a series of signifying strategies that make up the variety of texts on Doordarshan. It can be argued that an understanding of the media text can shed some light on the construction of the specific nation and national image, where the nation becomes, to some extent, a cultural product, produced by the media and around the media.

However, the ability and specificity of Doordarshan in creating an image of India is also determined by the transformations of the medium itself. Doordarshan in the seventies was separated between regions, with little linkage between regional broadcast centers. At that point, there was little possibility of Doordarshan being used to develop a national image. At best, it was a didactic medium with occasional entertainment spots. As I had pointed out in the first chapter, Doordarshan was primarily a regional medium. However, Doordarshan began to reach the entire nation after satellite and microwave connections were established during the ASIAD games. This is also the time when the role of television in producing a national image became critical. Consequently, the question of autonomy from Central government control also became important, as demonstrated in my earlier discussions on the history of the Prasar Bharati Bill to set up an independent and autonomous Indian Broadcasting Corporation. Given the pervasiveness of Doordarshan and its growing centrality in popular culture, the ruling governments were reluctant to give up control of the medium. This is what I pointed out in the first chapter.

Currently, the National Network of Doordarshan can reimage the country in a way that is informed by the ideology of the social bloc which has control of this non-autonomous medium. Particularly in the telecast of the *Mahabharat* serial, television in Indian culture was combined with a central Indian epic. This only reinforced the emerging dominant position of television in India (after all, it brought *Mahabharat* to every home), constantly redefining India as the bharat of Mahabharat. Thus it is the combination of the specific signifying strategies of television, and the importance of the *Mahabharat* serial, that redefines India on Doordarshan.

## *Doordarshan's India*

### Hindu India

What emerges is an image of India that is produced and reproduced by Doordarshan and circulated as the dominant and preferred one. This is clearly a Hindu image where the dominant religious practices are indeed Hindu-centric. It is the variety of signifying practices of Doordarshan that is able to achieve this.

Television serials, such as *Mahabharat* and *Ramayan*, have constantly projected Hindu religious rituals and ceremonies as the central issues of many of the episodes. Certain signifying strategies (such as the use of particular idols, the representation of Indian holy men and the image of Indian Gods and Goddesses) have been repetitively used in a variety of programs.

While *Mahabharat* and *Ramayan* were the two principal serials that were concerned with Hindu theology, there are a variety of other programs that have appeared after the two, which reinforce the Hindu-centricity of Doordarshan. Soon after *Mahabharat* went off the air, a shorter serial called *Krishna* was produced, which focused on the life of Krishna. Although not broadcast on Doordarshan, it was widely available on video and is now being telecast over the Metro Channel. Similarly, another serial, Karna, was produced, based on another character in the *Mahabharat*. This was shown for a short while on Sunday afternoons.

In all these serials, a certain set of similar signs have been used to signify Hindu religion. Most often these signs have been specific Hindu religious music, a particular set of religious rituals and other such semantic units that can be traced across a large range of programs, including programs which are not necessarily focused on a religious story. For example, the women in *Chehere* and *Chote Babu* perform similar religious rites for fertility and domestic harmony. They invoke the same Gods and Goddesses, using similar *mantras* and chants. Even though the religious ritual is not the central concern in some of these serials, the use of repetitive signifiers only reproduces a specific religious image of the nation.

Finally, the specificity of television lies in its pervasiveness and its segmented, yet repetitive, depiction of similar rituals. Even the temples in India cannot hope to reach everybody across the country with the same rituals. As I have pointed out earlier, religion and region are closely connected. However, the worship of Krishna in Uttar Pradesh is different from the tradition of worship in Karnataka. But, on National Network, the same image of Krishna is worshipped with the same offering and in the same way across the entire nation. This construction has many consequences.

First, other practices are marginalized and, within the national image, these are produced as deviant and non-Indian. This has resulted in a struggle that is no longer restricted to questions of specific religious rituals but is manifested in political struggle, where marginalized blocs attempt to reassert their differences with this Hindu center by actively seeking secession from it. This is precisely the challenge that Rajiv Gandhi faced when he became Prime Minister of India in 1985, following the assassination of his mother Indira Gandhi. This struggle is described by Rajiv:

> The first challenge was the unity and integrity of the country—there was Punjab, there was the problem in Tamil Nadu, there was a problem in Tripura with the TNLF [a local secessionist political party], there was a problem in Mizoram with the MNF trying to break away, the Darjeeling hills were simmering . . . so we had four or five areas where people were trying to break off . . . and Assam of course . . . so we had these parts of the country which were not at all happy and wanted to break away (Rajiv Gandhi in the documentary *Life and Death of a Dynasty*).

Some of these areas were geographically distant from the center in New Delhi, some were linguistically different from the Hindi hegemony, and some had a different dominant religion as, for example, Sikhism, in the case of Punjab. In its attempt to re-emphasize the dominance of the Hindu-Hindi alliance at the center, Doordarshan was able to trigger a struggle against this dominance, as the various elements in the country began to engage in an

ideological struggle that resulted in political instability and seces-
sionism. Within a reductionist argument of cause and effect, it may
be far-fetched to claim that Doordarshan was singlehandedly able
to cause these movements; indeed, these are areas that represent a
long-standing struggle in India.[6] However, within the conjunctural
and articulated image of societies and nations, Doordarshan plays
a crucial role in circulating an ideologically correct national Hindu
image and, consequently, generating an ideological struggle to
question and challenge those images and practices that marginalize
large parts of the social arena. This is a tight-rope that Doordarshan
was expected to walk in redefining India: on the one hand, to
promote a national image of unity and integration around the
Hindu-Hindi center and, at the same time, not to generate the
consequent ideological struggles that would result from this
dominance and subordination.

Another consequence of reproducing a Hindu India on Doordarshan was the increasing growth of Hindu fundamentalism in
India. Here, too, the key argument lies in the articulated nature of
practices. It is naive to claim that the circulation of Mahabharat on
Doordarshan led to the growth of Hindu fundamentalism in India.
However, it is important to recognize that the representation of
Ram, Krishna and the Pandavas in two major serials and other
programs described earlier, reproduced the residual Hindu practices
in India's cultural stock and memory. By bringing these characters
and their related practices back within popular culture and representing them as the preferred ones within popular culture, Doordarshan was able to establish the necessary links between the
production of a national image and Hindu religion. Within popular
culture, the recirculation of the Ramayan and Mahabharat brought
the Hindu heroes into the domesticity of nearly 90 per cent of
Indian homes, reemphasizing the Hinduness of India and, consequently, the unIndianness of non-Hindus.

A much sought for center was provided by Doordarshan when it
brought the characters of Ram and Krishna alive within the format
of the soap opera. Hinduism which always lacked such a center
within its multiplicity of Gods, was provided that center in the

---

[6] In describing the challenges faced by Nehru, the first Prime Minister of India,
one commentator argued: 'Nehru, the rational man, was trying to unify forces that
were vast, disparate and mystical.

characters of Ram and Krishna[7] on television. The consequences of this are felt in the emergence and quick growth of Hindu fundamentalism in India now. This is manifest at two levels: first, at the level of imaging the nation as a nation of Hindus and, secondly, in the political struggle where a particular political party—the Bharatiya Janata Party (BJP)—is able to call itself a Hindu party—a party that will be aware of the Hinduness of India and will reemphasize this Hinduness of India.

Therefore, in imaging the nation on Doordarshan, there is a growing sense of conceptualizing India as a Hindu country, moving it further away from the secular promises of the Constitution. Doordarshan has been able to use *Mahabharat* to tell the story of *Bharat*, a story that is closely related with the Hindu practices of the *bharat* of the Pandavas. Intellectuals in the country have been pointing this out. As one journalist states:

> But look at the use of government media to spread myth and magic like the episodes of *Mahabharat* and *Ramayan*. Let the mother teach her children the story of *Ramayan*. But to display it for a year on Doordarshan is really an opiate for illiterate and semi-literate people (Kushwant Singh, *India Today*, 15 May, 1991).

Numerous debates have constantly pointed this out.[8] Increasingly, India is moving towards a position where it is perceived as a nation that is predominantly a Hindu nation, where the official manifesto of secularism is increasingly weakened in favor of a national image as *bharat*—the Hindu nation. This is expressed in the words of a BJP member, Arun Jaitley, who refers to the BJP leader, L.K. Advani. Jaitley says, 'Mr Advani has said that even though he has not used the word Hindu, he would prefer that the word

[7] It is important to recognize a key difference between the Hindu religion and Christianity and Islam in this matter. Both Christianity and Islam have been able to claim a center in its development and perpetuation. In the case of Christianity, there is Jesus and the Pope, while in the case of Islam there is Muhammad. In the diversity of Hinduism there was no such central figure. However, Doordarshan, through *Ramayan* and *Mahabharat*, was able to provide these symbolic centers in Ram, Krishna and the Pandavas.

[8] One notable debate has been conducted by *India Today*, a fortnightly magazine of international circulation, that invited a large range of scholars to rethink the secular nature of India.

Hindu, Bharatiya (of Bharat) or Indian mean the same' (Jaitley, *India Today*, 15 May, 1991). This is precisely the articulation that television has been able to make. Doordarshan has been able to reproduce the residual connection between *bharat*, as the Hindu state at the time of the Mahabharat, and *bharat*, as the Hindu state poised on the brink of the twenty-first century.

This *bharat* is the vision of the BJP. The correspondence between Hindu practices and the political practices of the BJP is now complete. This is an ideological closure where the connection between the political party, the BJP, and the entire spectrum of Hindu practices is completed. This was achieved in a variety of ways, one of which was the mobilization of the practices that were reproduced and circulated by the 'religious soap operas' on television. *Ramayan*, in particular, was able to remind the Hindus of their lost center—in Ram. Using that as the central symbol, the BJP was able to articulate its own political struggles with a smaller group of Hindu fundamentalists who were struggling with the Muslims over the authenticity of a particular mosque in the north Indian Hindi-Hindu belt. The key to the struggle was that the mosque was supposedly built by the Muslim invader Babar to desecrate the exact location of Ram's birth in Ayodhya. The center provided by Doordarshan was now articulated with this issue, and Ram was reproduced in the Indian popular culture as the center of Hindu religion—whose loss is blamed on the Muslims, and whose 'authentic' birthplace now needs to be snatched away from the descendants of Babar, the Muslim invader.[9]

The arrival of *Mahabharat* on Doordarshan only reemphasized this, now articulating the representation of the story of the Pandavas with the story of *bharat*. The BJP was able to use these articulations in its political struggle, in challenging the dominance of the

[9] The significance of this is illustrated in the arguments of Yechuri who rightly argues that,

> The point at issue is that the people on the streets are not discussing the philosophical, epistemological or the ethical elements of Hinduism. They are discussing the right to existence and survival of people in the country on the basis of adherence to a certain religion (Yechuri, 1991).

This is precisely what is demonstrated in a Hindi slogan that in literal English translation means: tell the children of Babar that if they want to stay in *bharat* then they must remain Hindus.

Congress-led political center in New Delhi. The mobilization of this central figure of Ram is evident in the following lengthy quote describing the connections that are being drawn between the BJP as a political entity, and *bharat* as an imagined Hindu nation—one that will be produced by the BJP, if they are elected into power in the current elections.[10] The following description of the publicity methods of the BJP well illustrate the use of Ram as a central Hindu figure:

> An important vote bank is the youth. The party is hammering on the message that Ram equals unity and stability. Among the many campaign knick-knacks are paper caps with the slogan: 'I am proud of my cultural heritage' stamped on it. Caps are a clever idea for more than one reason: they will keep away the scorching heat and the sun and hopefully be bringing in the votes. The BJP strategists seem to have got their inspiration from the Pepsi advertisements of using caps. Moreover, there are stickers with the same slogans and with the added sentence: 'I shall vote BJP'. Other accessories to be sprinkled along the campaign trail are bangles with Sita-Ram written on them (Jain and Rahman, *India Today*, 15 May, 1991).

What Doordarshan broadcast as a 'religious soap opera' *(Ramayan)* was able to mobilize the political campaign that is now on hand in India, and indeed redefine the Indian image itself.

In summary, Doordarshan was able to reproduce the Hindu practices as dominant in imaging *bharat*. Moreover, it provided, in the narratives, the central Hindu figures around which discourses developed thus reimaging India as *bharat*—the Hindu state. Within the popular culture, the notion of a Hindu state— a *Hindutva*—is now dominant. It is articulated with being Indian, as well as being progressive. The question of religion is now articulated with the unquestioned and unequivocal preferred image of the popular culture of India.[11] The dominant image of the nation in the popular

[10] The elections of May 1991 were in progress, when this work was in the writing phase. However, voting was held up by the untimely assassination of Rajiv Gandhi.

[11] This articulation is evident in an *India Today* article, where the illustrating cartoon shows an executive, with a Personal Computer on his desk, who has a picture of Ram hanging on the wall with the blurb 'Ram-bow'. The executive is speaking on the phone and saying, 'What's wrong with Ram? After all, he was the original yuppie . . . he was a prince.'

culture is indeed this—one that articulates the majority with a particular religion. And Doordarshan was able to provide the representations and circulate them within the popular culture. Moreover, this religion is also connected with the Hindi language.

## Hindi India

Anderson has pointed out that a nation can be imagined around a language[12]. In the case of India, Hindi and Hinduism are also closely related. As I had pointed out earlier, Hindi is an off-shoot of Sanskrit. The latter is considered to be the quintessential Hindu language in which all the primary Hindu texts were composed. Consequently, Hindi is also connected with Hinduism. On Doordarshan this connection is emphasized by using Hindi as the language of serials (such as *Mahabharat* and *Ramayan*) that concern Hindu religious figures and practices. On a broader note, the National Network programs on Doordarshan constantly reproduce Hindi as the national language and there is a tendency to reaffirm that Hindi ought to be the national language. This is done by choosing Hindi as the language of broadcast for the majority of the National Network programs on Doordarshan.[13]

Almost all programs emanating from Delhi are in Hindi. Among them, some are key broadcasts, such as the Hindi news which precedes the English news in the evening on prime-time television. The English news is nearly a verbatim translation of the Hindi

[12] Anderson stresses the question of language as a discursive practice around which nations are built, thought and imagined. It is also possible that a nation can be imagined around other practices which are not necessarily restricted to language. Anderson elaborates thus at the very beginning of the book:

What I am proposing is that nationalism has to be understood by aligning it, not with self-consciously held political ideologies, but with the large cultural systems that preceded it, out of which—as well as against which—it came into being (Anderson, 1983).

Here Anderson makes the point that a nation has to be understood through a set of cultural systems. These cultural systems are made up of a set of practices, for instance, language.

[13] A news item in a recent *India Today* indicates that Mandi House required that the lyrics of an advertisement spot on the National Network be changed from Goanese to Hindi since Hindi and English were the only two languages that were supposed to be used in advertisements.

news, with the same footage and news items. Most of the educational programs are in Hindi. Entertainment programs, like serials and sports telecasts, are mostly in Hindi also. Interestingly, when a program is in a different language, there is always a special name given to it to differentiate it from other programs. Thus, in the 'TV Guide' section of newspapers and magazines, a serial such as *Chote Babu* is not described as a 'Hindi serial' while an Oriya program will have a name that distinguishes the language of broadcast. Through this process, the Hindi language is constantly reproduced as the natural and expected language of television broadcast in India. For instance, Hindi feature films are not described as 'Hindi' films, but a Bengali cinema telecast on the National Network will be called a 'Bengali feature film'.

Consequently, other languages are produced as non-national and specific to regions in the country. Thus a non-Hindi program on Doordarshan is often also described by a secondary text, such as television guides in newspapers, as a program from a particular part of India. The inseparable connection between languages and regions are thus reproduced in imaging India on Doordarshan.

## North Indian India

As I have already pointed out, the primary part of India that is reproduced in television serials is north-central India, which is also often called the Hindu-Hindi belt. Some Hindu religious programs, such as *Mahabharat, Ramayan* and *Krishna* are set against the background of a mythical north India in and around such ancient cities as Hastinapur and Ayodhya. However, in other programs like family melodramas and serials such as *Rajni* and *Chote Babu*, the location is not already defined in an epic, yet the stories are set against a background of north-central India. Here a choice is being made to place the stories in a specific undefined city or village, whose only defining characteristic is its location in a recognizable part of India.

Furthermore, it is only Doordarshan that can successfully accomplish this since it can repeat these sets in a variety of texts across a period of time. Television is not spatially bound as theater or *yatra*, which is played out against the background of the region where it is being acted out. On television, the background can be signified in specific ways just as the material activities of the people in the background can also be reproductive of a selected region.

In summary, the leadership of a north Indian social bloc is in opposition with the non-Hindu and non-Hindi blocs in the country. Needless to say, the latter have their own set of practices that produce popular culture in various parts of India. For instance, non-Hindi speaking southern India represents a wealth of cultural practices that are different from north Indian culture. However, this difference is reproduced in *Ramayan* in a way that reduces south Indian culture as subordinate. As one commentator(a south Indian highcaste Hindu) has pointed out, the *Ramayan* consistently reproduces any practice of southern India as the practices of apes, all in alliance with Ram but subordinate to Ram—who is a product of north Indian Hindu culture[14] Doordarshan, has been able to reproduce these regional images and recirculate the dominance of the hegemonic center.

Doordarshan's India is thus an India that would be better called *bharat*, where the central cultural practices are those that revolve around Hinduism and the language is predominantly Hindi. This reproduction has now been able to mobilize a new political conservatism that is the Hindu right. The images reproduced and circulated by Doordarshan have now indeed become dominant in India's popular culture. The consequent struggles can only get acute and bloody now that the precarious balance between communal harmony in national integration, and the dominance of the majority Hindus, has swayed to the right.

Doordarshan is able to position itself in two ways with these struggles. First, Doordarshan is able to represent a set of practices as the preferred national practices in India, thus representing, reproducing and circulating these images as the preferred national images.[15] Secondly, Doordarshan is also able to articulate the

[14] Sitaram Yechuri, the south Indian intellectual points to this in saying, 'All through ingrained in our consciousness is that, in *Ramayan*, every single king south of the Vindhyas [a mountain range that geographically divides the north and south India] is depicted as an animal' (Yechuri, 1991).

[15] This is a conjunctural argument that focuses on specific historic moments when specific dominant social and cultural practices have been represented on the media, aiding in the circulation of a specific dominant image of the nation. A variety of authors have made this argument in their works on various national media. Notable are the work on *Dallas* (Ang, 1985; Katz and Liebes, 1987; Newcomb, 1987; Silj, 1988), the work of Chaney (1986) on British television. Bennett and Woollacott

practices of television—of watching television—as a dominant national practice, thus establishing its legitimate position in the chain of practices that are articulated together in describing the national image.[16] Thus, by representing Hindu practices on *Mahabharat* and by articulating the practice of watching *Mahabharat* as a religious practice, Doordarshan is able to doubly determine what is being produced as the dominant, unquestioned and preferred practices in India today.

However, it is not necessarily a harmonious picture that emerges, even on Doordarshan. A nation, particularly India, is riddled with internal contradictions and struggles, and its imaging on television also cannot help but reproduce that. In spite of the ways in which Doordarshan has been reproducing a specific national image, particularly in its National Network broadcasts, there are a variety of signifying practices that question this emergent hegemony. Indeed, there are a number of programs on Doordarshan that question the hegemony of the Hindi-Hindu center. These programs, and the manner in which they question the dominance of Hindu and Hindi positions, is the issue that I shall examine in the next chapter.

---

(1987) in regarding Bond as the representation of the British tradition, and Turner (1988) on Australian cinema, Chakravarty (1987) on Indian film, Hay (1987a) on Italian cinema, Elsaesser (1989) on German film, and Fiske (1987a) on television in USA.

[16] A particular medium, or even a particular text (for instance, a film like *Crocodile Dundee*, or a TV show such as *Dallas*) reproduces and circulates a specific dominant national image because certain articulations exist between the medium (or text) and certain dominant practices that help to image the 'nation'. This argument is made by authors such as Chambers (1986) and Brundson and Morley (1981) about various programs on BBC. Frith's (1978) work on music, and the practices of social groups, can also be extrapolated to make a similar argument about national practices, among which watching television is critical in India.

# 7

# In Conclusion: Doordarshan: Its Internal Contradictions and Position in Everyday Life

> 'Jai Shri Ram, Bharat Mata Ki Jai' [Victory for Lord Ram, Victory for Mother India] is how she begins her campaign speech, a clenched fist raised to illustrate her new ideology. Deepika, 26, also has a clever—and catchy—way of getting around the language problem: 'I will address you in the language you hear me speaking on TV'. In Padra (in non-Hindi speaking Gujarat), a 15,000 strong crowd braved the scorching May heat for hours just for a real-life 'darshan' [a divine vision] of the telegoddess.
>
> **India Today**, 15 May 1991, describing the campaign strategy of BJP candidate, Deepika Chikhalia, the star who played Sita (Ram's consort) in Ramayan.

**I shall use** this last chapter as a point to investigate two issues that arise out of the earlier discussions and then provide a few closing remarks. The central focus of this work has been to investigate the role of television in India's popular culture using the method of textual analysis. What emerges out of this study are a set of related questions and a reexamination of some of the various vectors that produce India's popular culture (namely, religion, region, language and gender).

By looking at the *Mahabharat* serial it can be established that the text and the medium are increasingly producing a popular culture, where the dominant articulations are between Hinduism, Hindi, northern India and a male patriarchy. The production of an articulated hegemonic leadership of this particular social bloc is precisely the role of television in India's popular culture now. There are two other issues that need to be examined.

First, this hegemony is not uncontested. Indeed, texts on Doordarshan itself are contradictory. While 'religious soap operas' are reproducing the Hindu-Hindi hegemony, there are a variety of other texts that remain in a contradictory relation with this hegemony. It is true that these other texts have not been quite as effective in reshaping the popular culture of India, but their existence needs to be recognized and these texts have to be placed in relation with the hegemonic national image being produced by Doordarshan.[1]

The second issue that needs to be considered is the position of television within the everyday material practices of the people who are watching it. This is legitimately a question of audience analysis and ethnography. However, it is necessary to rethink the way in which television has been articulated with the everyday practices of the viewers of television. Given the extent of diversity of the audience, this is indeed a gigantic task. However, it is possible to make certain judgments about the way in which Doordarshan has been able to redefine the domestic space, rhythm and practices of the bulk of the Indian people. These are the two issues that I will be addressing in the first part of this chapter.

## The Contradictions on Doordarshan

It is true that Doordarshan has been closely related with a Hindu-Hindi bloc. Numerous critiques have repeatedly pointed out the

---

[1] The example of *aka Pavlo*—an unsuccessful serial on American television—is a good simile for the failed programs on Doordarshan too. These programs, arguably, did not represent or articulate what was being produced and circulated as the national practices of India at specific moments in time.

close relationship between the medium and a Hindu hegemony which has successfully reproduced its practices in the texts of Doordarshan, particularly *Mahabharat* and *Ramayan*.[2] However, this has not been a process that has been free of contradictions. A variety of other texts have been circulated on Doordarshan that do not necessarily reproduce this Hindu-Hindi hegemony but have attempted to reproduce the practices of other social and religious blocs within the country and present other cultural, religious and social practices that have been systematically marginalized by the Hindu programs. These texts have spanned a great length in time and belong to a variety of genres, from serialized soap operas to talk shows.[3] The primary contradictions that have been addressed are the ones around religion, region and gender. Given the articulated nature of these contradictions, none works in isolation. All these contradictions are articulated with the fourth locus of stress— language. Thus the struggles and their representation are articulated together.

One key feature of these texts on Doordarshan has been the attempt to rethink the primary religious contradiction in popular Indian culture—the Hindu-Muslim conflictual relation. This has been a historically violent relationship, where no position of mutual coexistence has been found except for a few provisional ones.[4] Indeed, a variety of other struggles have been articulated with the religious question, while making the religious issue the primary one. This has also often been a violent and bloody struggle.[5] One

---

[2] As Das Gupta points out about the first religious soap opera to arrive on Doordarshan: 'It's [*Ramayan*] direct appeal to Hindu revivalism was well hidden within the fame of the epic which proved to be sheep's clothing for the communal wolf' (Das Gupta, 1990).

[3] From the early days of television in India, there have been non-Hindi transmissions and texts that have questioned the authenticity and legitimacy of the Hindi-Hindu hegemony. Some of these texts have been used as illustrative examples here.

[4] For instance, the uneasy peace between warring Muslim and Hindu factions in Calcutta following Partition was largely orchestrated by the powerful presence of Mahatma Gandhi in Calcutta, who threatened a fast unto death if the religious groups did not make peace. This peace lasted for a while, but violent confrontations between Muslims and Hindus in Calcutta is a matter of routine.

[5] Perhaps the bloodiest of the religious struggles have been the ones that followed the Partition of the subcontinent into India and Pakistan, where there was a mass exodus of Hindus from Pakistan, and Muslims from India. This resulted in violent riots in bordering states such as West Bengal and Punjab.

program, *Tamas*, made an attempt to reconsider this relationship and present what could have been a progressive step towards examining the differences between the blocs. From the textual perspective, this program stood out as different from the Hindu 'religious soap operas,' with their persistent recirculation of Hindu practices. Indeed, no specific religious ideology became central in this narrative; indeed, it was the struggle between the religions that was reproduced in this text.

*Tamas* represents the practices in Indian life that have triggered the violence between Hindus and Muslims. The entire narrative is set in the tumultuous period following independence and Partition. The first episode of the story revolves around a set of practices that lead to violent rioting between Hindus and Muslims. While the narrative is not necessarily reproductive of either of the religious practices, it does remind the reader of the contradictions in our popular culture, and the futility of their resolution in violence. The prevailing themes in this serial are violence, communalism and the terrors associated with communal violence that is a mainstay of India's everyday life. Indeed, as one commentator points out, the strength of *Tamas*, and Doordarshan, lies precisely here: in representing that violence at a time when the entire image of India as a nation was being questioned in view of the struggles of the marginalized against the dominating center. In the words of Ghosh:

> In a way, we have forgotten history and its lessons. So we are learning anew the meaning of violence, terrorism, communal sentiments in Punjab, West Bengal, Gujarat . . . name any state. That is why the featuring of *Tamas* over Doordarshan is so important (Ghosh, 1988).

This is precisely what has often been described as the period of *glastnost* on Doordarshan, when Doordarshan was able to circulate texts that contradicted the hegemonic position that was being mobilized by texts such as *Mahabharat*.

The primary reason why *Tamas* became crucial in rethinking the position of Doordarshan is because its story did not have its roots in Hindu practices but actually explored the violent modality of the Hindu-Muslim relationship. This was a move away from the ever-increasing Hindu articulation of Doordarshan. In fact, as one media watcher in India points out: 'Indeed, *Tamas* is also important in that the vital subject of the Hindu-Muslim relationship had remained untouched ever since Sathyu's remarkable portrait of it in *Garam Hawa*' (Das Gupta, 1988). This internal contradiction on Doordarshan only reproduces the tensions that exist in India's popular culture, where there are several issues that do not fit into the homogeneous construction of Hindu India.

Other texts have also exhibited a tendency to move away from this pervasive Hindu hegemony. For example, Behula Chowdhury points out that the serial *Kabir*, based on the life of a non-Hindu prophet of the same name, reproduced Hindu-Muslim differences in a way where one religion was not subordinated to the other. In fact, it explored the relationship between the religions in progressive ways. In her words:

> Less garish and melodramatic than *Ramayan*, it [*Kabir*] also seems slightly more researched. The emphasis on the common concerns of the Hindu and the Muslims (poverty is universal, we have one enemy, the rich) is unavoidable and presented with considerable restraint (Chowdhury, 1987c).

While the commentator is concerned about the representation of struggle between economic classes, she does recognize the way in which the serial is able to represent the relations between the Muslims and Hindus, a factor that is non-existent within the texts of *Mahabharat* and *Ramayan*.

Moving away from the vector of religion, the National Network has also circulated texts that question other conflicting relations within India's popular culture. Serials such as *Rajni* and *Kasauti* have questioned the gendered and regional structure of India's popular culture. *Rajni*, in particular, has been able to represent the emergent position of women within India's popular culture by textually representing the variety of practices of domination that constantly reinsert the Indian woman into patriarchal hegemony. *Kasauti* brought to Doordarshan 'unpleasant realities in different parts of the country' (Ghosh, 1988).[6]

In *Rajni*, the housewife, Rajni successfully questions oppressive practices and emerges redefining herself and the gender position

---

[6] This serial was considered to be particularly bold. It was regarded as an example of the temporary opening up of the textual and ideological boundaries of Doordarshan in the late eighties.

within the structures of domination. It is this gendered victory that also becomes the locus of suspicion of television's effectivity in popular culture. The following citation from Das Gupta illustrates the way in which Rajni the housewife and *Rajni* the serial are both received as unnatural representations of gender relations, as well as closely articulated with a variety of social and cultural practices:

> It [*Rajni*] introduced TV's brand of fantasy by having her win every fight against the dishonest doctor, the school principal greedy for donations, the lazy postal peon, the grocer cheating on weights and so on. When she turned her fury on unscrupulous taxi drivers, they came out in protest against what they saw as calumny against them (Das Gupta, 1990).

This not only represents a variety of contradictions but also represents the struggle of gender with a diversity of forces, all of which also represent a male hegemony. In reproducing these conflicts in the text and resolving the conflict in a way where the female comes out as the winner, the medium is able to redefine gender relations and positions in the structures and relations of India's popular culture. It is called 'fantasy' precisely because it is unnatural and thus continues an ideological struggle with the naturalized male hegemony. This is the locus of an ideological struggle where a particular set of articulations are being questioned and a new set of articulations are being produced with the ultimate movement being in a progressive direction, and contrary to the articulations being produced by texts such as *Mahabharat*.

This is also seen in the case of regional broadcasts, where particular television stations have reproduced regional practices to set them up in contrast to the naturalized national practices. This contradiction is made apparent in the case of the Calcutta station which devoted a lot of time to bringing the works of the poet Rabindranath Tagore to the viewer, but the central broadcast did not pay much attention to it.[7] Similarly, Calcutta station's weekly

[7] Indeed, this signifying practice is articulated with the popular cultural practices in the state of West Bengal, where Tagore is a vibrant element in the popular culture. Bengalis, in general, consider Tagore to be a central figure in their popular culture.

women's program, *Ghare Baire*,[8] is able to appropriate, within its text, issues and conflicts that have now become crucial in India's cultural arena. In describing one episode of the program, Behula Chowdhury writes:

> *Ghare Baire* is one of the few departments of Calcutta Doordarshan that does not fall back on used goods. This week the program hostess interviewed couples who defied caste, provincial and religious barriers to make happy and harmonious marriages (Chowdhury, 20 June, 1987).

Here, several contradictions in Indian society are examined, and questioned, thus representing the variety of contradictory relationships that produce India's popular culture. Most of the *Ghare Baire* programs touch upon issues such as this, primarily concentrating on the question of gender roles and relations. There are, thus, a variety of texts and genres that are not articulated with the practices of the hegemonic center. These texts and genres have attempted to first question that center, and then reproduce practices that rearticulate new relations between the various straining forces.

Several conclusions can be drawn from the variety of examples that are discussed here. Doordarshan is not a seamless cultural formation,[9] as would appear when examining some of the more popular texts on the medium. While *Mahabharat* and *Ramayan* reproduce a specifically Hindu hegemony, there are a variety of other texts that question this hegemony and open it up for reappraisal. The various contradictions that are smoothed over, and the social blocs that are marginalized by the 'religious soap operas' (and some other Hindi and Hindu centered texts), are drawn back within the television formation by these other texts.

This opens up the possibility of television playing an alternative role in India's popular culture. It not only describes the nation, and the practices of the nation, as Hindu, but also opens up the

---

[8] Interestingly, named after a play by Tagore, where he investigates the position of women in the structure of Bengali society, ultimately providing his heroine with a path of escape from patriarchal oppression. This illustrates the variety of ways in which local stations are able to link together, in an articulated chain, a large set of elements in describing the modality of the regional practices of the Calcutta station.

[9] A seamless cultural formation is one which appears to be free of internal contradictions. This is a near impossibility unless under totalitarian conditions.

possibility of alternative practices contesting this national image. It is out of these struggles that, ultimately, a different national image can be obtained. To a certain extent, this is the aim of national integration, where a variety of practices, in combination, produce a national identity. This is precisely what Das Gupta suggests in saying: '*Tamas* is thus unique in more ways than one. Taken with Ramesh Sharma's carefully crafted *Kasauti*, it may be the turning point in Doordarshan's uneven struggle to live up to its legitimate aims' (Das Gupta, 1988). The legitimate aim is to reproduce the struggles in India's popular culture, and provide access to the variety of voices and practices that are struggling to find a place in the national image.

The cultural formation of Doordarshan is indeed riddled with internal inconsistencies which are produced around the chief vectors discussed earlier—religion, region, language and gender. Door-darshan has reproduced the practices related with other religions, particularly Islam, and has questioned the practices that set up the contradictions between religions. This has not happened in a smooth or uncontested manner. The production and circulation of non-Hindu serials (like *The Sword of Tipu Sultan*) have been contested and threatened. Indeed, the authenticity of this serial is questioned in the opening sequence when a voice-over reminds the viewer that the serial is 'fiction'. On the other hand, the legitimacy and authenti-city of the Hindu serials have never been questioned. In fact, the success of *Ramayan* encouraged the appearance of *Mahabharat*. As Das Gupta points out:

> His [Ramanand Sagar, the producer of *Ramayan*] *Ramayan* prompted the arrival of *Mahabharat* on the scene, made by B.R. Chopra, a better known filmmaker in every respect. He, however, was quick to see which side the bread was buttered and played up the religious aspects of a mainly secular epic in a variety of devious ways (Das Gupta, 1990).

This is precisely how the struggle continues on Doordarshan between serials such as the *Sword of Tipu Sultan* and *Mahabharat*.

In a similar way, the contradictions between regions have been reproduced in the differences between the regional programs and the national broadcasts. The legitimacy of languages and practices that are different from the Hindi center have been emphasized in the regional programs coming out of the various regional broadcast centers. The need for a second channel of transmission in some metropolitan areas, such as Calcutta, is often generated by the question of language, and the ubiquitous presence of Hindi on the National Network. In referring to the predominance of Bengali on the regional second channel in Calcutta, Chowdhury points out, 'The emphasis is understandable and even desirable, for the network is not going to look after the language for us' (Chowdhury, 15 January, 1988).

Yet, the issue is not that linear, because the same author is quick to point out that in the struggle between Hindi, and regional languages such as Bengali, a common unifying language—English— is getting increasingly marginalized: 'But English language programs have become increasingly infrequent . . . . The Second Channel could provide non-Bengali viewers with something they could enjoy in a different language' (Chowdhury, 15 January, 1988).

This illustrates the complexity of the articulations between language and the medium. And Doordarshan has become the locus of this struggle, attempting to challenge the linguistic hegemony of Hindi by finding opportunities, as in the second channel, where that hegemony can be contested.

The gender roles and positions that are being naturalized within the patriarchal hegemony of the Hindu nation are being questioned in rearticulating the gender in progressive ways. The gender position being mobilized and circulated by the Hindu epics is questioned by the programs that attempt to reproduce a different set of gender relations and positions.

In this manner, television has been both the locus and a party to the ideological struggle to remap and reimage India. However, this hegemonic struggle has been increasingly moving towards the Hindu right. The dominant images of nation and national popular practices are increasingly articulated to Hindu fundamentalist practices. This is evident to most observers of the media, as Dasgupta points out:

> Mr Das Gupta said the way in which the epics, Mahabharat and Ramayan, had been treated on television had destroyed their universality, had desecularized them and had made them into instruments of religious fundamentalism. He was of the view

that *Mahabharat* on television showed religion to occupy a
central position, something the epic does not suggest (Staff, *The
Telegraph*, 1990).

This only suggests that the ideological struggle on television is
increasingly being lost to the fundamentalists. This struggle is then
articulated with the current political struggles, as pointed out in
earlier chapters.

The key point to note here is that there is a struggle continuing
on and around Doordarshan. The medium is not a monolithic
uncontradictory apparatus of hegemony that is unchallenged,
either within, or outside, its textual practices. This is precisely why
it is important to examine the medium carefully, and perhaps
provide the demystification that has been attempted in this project.
The existence of these differences do not, in any way, make
programs like *Mahabharat* and *Ramayan* any less threatening. The
contradictions only retain the space for negotiation, and questioning of this emerging hegemony.

Doordarshan, as a cultural formation, is also located in an
articulated relationship with the variety of internal struggles existing in India now. The notion of formation assumes this articulation,
where the representations on television only reproduce and reshape
the ongoing struggles in the popular cultural spaces. The struggles
over representation are also articulated with the variety of everyday
practices with which the medium is articulated. As Fiske has
pointed out, it is this articulation of the medium, with the different
practices that produce popular culture, that makes the role of
television crucial in the understanding of popular culture.

It is, therefore, important to investigate the variety of ways in
which Doordarshan is positioned, in relation to other practices,
within the everyday life of the variety of conflicting social blocs in
India. This is the second issue that I will investigate in this chapter.
The textual practices of Doordarshan, as well as the practice of
watching television, are articulated with the variety of material
practices in everyday life, and it is this articulation that implicates
the position of television in popular culture, as well as the way in
which television becomes a significant part of the contradictory
practices of everyday life.

## Doordarshan and Everyday Life

It has increasingly been recognized that television is a medium that enters the domestic private spaces of everyday life, unlike cinema, or the more traditional forms of mass communication. Like radio, television is able to articulate its signifying practices, as well as the practice of watching television with a range of different domestic practices. The influence is on domestic practices and, in households, precisely because television is watched in houses, in homes. As Morley and Silverstone point out: 'Why Households? In one sense the answer is a simple one. We watch television in our homes. The household and the family is our primary environment' (Morley and Silverstone, 1988). This is precisely the way that television is watched in India too. It is within the household, however complex that notion is, that television is watched.[10] Television is watched in the living room, in the bedroom and in the company of other members of the household.

The extent of this articulation is determined somewhat by the sophistication of the technology. For instance, in the United States and parts of Western Europe, the television set, or the 'monitor,' often works as a video display unit for the home computer, or the site where video games are played. This has become increasingly evident in the displacement of television technology into uses that go beyond the reception of broadcast programs. As Morley and Silverstone point out:

> There is a history of displacement in media technologies in the household, but the displacement is neither complete nor simple. Radio survives. Videos and computers and cables are plugged into the television, converting it into a VDU or an instrument for narrowcasting or interactive communication (Morley and Silverstone, 1988).

[10] Morley and Silverstone also illustrate the sophistication and the complex thinking of the family and the household. While their interest is primarily in the household in Britain, I am more concerned with households in India. However, in both cases it needs to be recognized that the household is getting to be an increasingly complex institution which, as Morley and Silverstone point out; 'the domestic is neither a simple nor an unproblematic category' (Morley and Silverstone, 1988).

In India, on the other hand, the television set still remains primarily an instrument whose use is restricted to the reception of broadcast signals from television stations. Only recently has the presence of video record players in homes increased. Grassroot level cable systems in apartment buildings have also emerged. As an *India Today* feature points out:

> When cable TV started in Bombay eight years ago, it was confined largely to posh multi-storeyed building complexes. In recent years, however, it has changed from a 'class' phenomenon to a 'mass' one. In Dharavi [a relatively low income area of Bombay] alone, at least a dozen operators have come up in the last few months. Says Srinivas Naidu, one such operator: 'You can have all the advantages of a VCR without owning one' (Staff, *India Today*, November 1990).

All this represents a considerable sophistication of technology, but compared to the possibilities and potential, it is clearly one still in its infancy, and restricted to the urban areas. In spite of the emergence of these technologies, I would argue, the primary use of the television set is still in the reception of broadcasts off the air.

Another factor that determines the way in which television is articulated within the everyday practices of domestic life is the economic affluence of a particular social bloc. Again, in many parts of Western Europe, and particularly in the United States, the television set is increasingly affordable, resulting in the existence of multiple television sets in a home. As Morley and Silverstone have suggested, the family center around the television could be displaced in some situations, where every person can retract into the private space of private entertainment cells, with the personalized television screen as the center of this entertainment space. This is combined with the fact that there are a large variety of uses that the set can be put to, as well as a large choice of program material that is available in Western countries, which have a longer history of television. This results in a redefinition of domestic relations and interactions. In India, however, the cost related to television receivers still makes it uneconomical to maintain multiple sets within a household. Most often there is just one television set, and this also carries a limited choice of programs—one channel only.[11] Thus there is little to choose from, and one television set is often the rule.

It is within this scenario of a single television set for a household, with a single channel of broadcast, that it is necessary to consider the position of television in the everyday practices of India. There are, however, a few more points that need to be made, specifically in terms of India. First, the medium is a relatively new phenomenon in India. The way it was inserted within the practices of popular culture in the early seventies is vastly different from the way it is inserted now. Indeed, in the early years of television, its novelty appeal far exceeded any other role that it could play in the popular culture. People watched television precisely because it was something new. However, with time, the position of television changed, and it became a naturalized center of social and cultural practices in the household. It was no longer a 'new' medium, but became a part of everyday life. This is the role of television that I shall discuss, rather than enter into a historic discussion of the changes.

Secondly, the question of 'family' itself is a complex and contra- dictory notion in India, worthy of a thesis by itself. However, the key point to make is that the family, as an institution, has seen major changes in the past two decades at the time when television was also becoming increasingly accessible. The traditional family, consisting of a large number of members living within the same household as a 'joint family,' has seen disintegration. 'Nuclear families' (where a couple·and their children live together) are on the increase.[12] The traditional role of the woman in the family has changed rapidly too: from the quintessential mother-wife role to the mother-wife-wage-earner role. This has affected relations within

[11] At the time of writing (1992), some cities such as Calcutta and New Delhi saw the appearence of a second channel, leading to some choice for the viewer. However, this was restricted to only the metropolitan areas. Also, in the bordering states, such as West Bengal and Punjab, there was a tendency to tune into the Bangladesh and Pakistani broadcasts respectively. Thus, for the majority of viewers the choice was restricted to the single channel of broadcast. But following 1992, there has been a rapid growth in television technology and software, with the availability of multiple channels via cable, and the viewer has the choice of watch- ing a large variety of programs, including those put out by satellite broadcasters such as Star TV.

[12] Consequently, there is a redefinition of domestic space—an issue that I will take up presently.

the family as well.[13] With the increase of nuclear families amongst working couples, domestic space is shrinking to smaller apartment houses and single family homes in cities and suburbs. The urban domestic sphere of interaction is now limited to parents, children and a servant, instead of numerous brothers, sisters, aunts, uncles and a large collection of servants who would all live together. These changes are implicated by, and implicate, the role television is playing in everyday life too.

A third and final point to note about television in India is that it is extremely difficult to pin down the exact nature of the audience. Given the immense diversity of social blocs, it is a mammoth task to arrive at a unanimous description of the audience. Most audience research has chosen to focus on the urban middle class, who also happen to be the largest owners of individual television sets. In spite of the early hopes of television becoming the center and medium for rural education and reform, television has indeed become a medium of, and for, the urban middle class. As Das Gupta points out,

> This dewey-eyed vision of a community set in each village that would bring about a social revolution at the grassroots is a thing of the past. Experience soon showed that electronic equipment was hard to maintain outside metro cities, not to speak of places where even handpumps were not repaired for months and years, and women and children had to haul water all day from long distances. So, despite pious wishes, TV, like water, found its own level—in middle class home (Das Gupta, 1990).

This is the bloc which has the economic conditions to own individual and private television sets in their homes. The rural audience is more dependant on the community television in a village hall. Indeed, the ethnographic study of Hartmann, Patil and Dighe (1989), of four villages of India, emphasizes that television plays a minor role in rural practices. Within the rural bloc, it is the radio and newspapers that are still popular. It is therefore difficult, without performing extensive ethnographic research, to arrive at

[13] The consequent change in domestic time, leisure and rhythm needs to be considered too.

reliable conclusions about the complex ways in which television is inserted into the everyday practices of the variety of viewers in India. However, given my own urban middle-class cultural background, and the evidence that urban social blocs are emerging as the primary viewers, I shall describe the ways in which the medium has been inserted within the everyday practices of this social bloc only. This social bloc is primarily represented by nuclear families and a few joint families that make up the bulk of the urban population. This is a considerable bulk too; for instance the population of Calcutta is now nearly ten million people, a large proportion of whom are watching television, participating in other cultural practices and making political decisions.

In examining the way in which television is inserted in the everyday practices of the urban bloc there are two primary issues that I shall examine. First, I shall consider the ways in which the domestic space of families has been redefined by television. This will be followed by an examination of the ways in which domestic time, leisure and the rhythms of domestic life have been reshaped by television. These vectors represent the two primary ways in which television is able to play a part in the redefinition of its role in domestic everyday practices.

The notion of domestic space and spheres, and how it has been implicated by the introduction of the electronic media, has been the focus of research in the West for some time (see, for instance, Lull, 1988; Morley, 1980; Morley and Silverstone, 1988). The primary conclusions drawn out of this research indicate that domestic space and spheres are indeed redefined by the introduction of media such as radio and television. As Moores (1988) has pointed out, radio seemed to occupy a 'natural' position in the private spheres of households. This is one of the key aspects of the way in which the electronic media has been able to redefine domestic spaces. A medium such as television has been accepted as a natural element in domestic space. The practice of watching television in India is no longer something that people consider unnatural, special or novel. It has been taken for granted, and the physical presence of the television set in the living room or bedroom is unquestioned. Watching television is now a natural act, and domestic space is designed around this natural act. Among the various texts on Doordarshan, *Mahabharat* became a text that was taken for granted. The always-already text had a 'natural' appeal for the majority of viewers. Therefore, watching *Mahabharat* was quickly naturalized within the everyday practices of most of India, in an unquestioned and uncontradictory manner.

The notion of space, however, needs to be thought of in two ways. First, in terms of geographic space, where the television enters the living room or the bedroom and redescribes the way that space is used. For example, in India, the television is usually placed in the living room, thus redescribing the way in which the space is organized around the special center of the television. All domestic activity in the living room is now concentrated around the television set. In this manner, the living room, which might not have necessarily been the center of household activity, is now made the center by the introduction of the television set. This is the geographic space where the family now interacts with, and around, the television set, and around the practices of watching television. The physical presence of the television set is articulated with conversation, with family interaction, and often the resolution of family tensions and contradictions. This is precisely the site where several family members congregate to watch *Mahabharat* and rethink, not only their relations with each other, but with the text too. In this space the tertiary text is generated, where the primary text on the screen is reread in terms of conversation about the text. In the case of *Mahabharat*, the tertiary texts often re-produce the Hinduness of the primary text, reemphasizing and recirculating, in the mode of gossip, the Hindu practices that are represented in *Mahabharat*. Indeed, in some instances, the notion of tertiary 'practices' extended to a worship of the television set with flowers and incense when the serial was broadcast.

The domestic sphere also has to be considered in a second way: as a cultural and social sphere where interactions occur. This is no longer the geographic space of the living room or the bedroom, but the arena where household conflicts are played out. This is also the sphere which is distinct from public spheres. From this perspective, too, television has been able to redefine the private sphere of domestic interaction. As Morley and Silverstone point out:

> leisure time has increasingly been located within the home, as
> opposed to within the public sphere—the street, or in the pub,
> or cinema—as one in which broadcasting itself played a key

role, by increasing the attractiveness of the home as a site for leisure (Morley and Silverstone, 1988).

Although the authors refer to the context of Britain, this is precisely what has happened in the redefinition of the domestic sphere in India. In India, where the public sphere used to be the center of leisure,[14] the household has now become the center of leisure activities. Doordarshan has now been taken for granted within that sphere, where the entire family is now brought together on Sunday mornings to watch *Mahabharat*. Perhaps the only other practice that has a similar ability to reshape the domestic sphere are religious ceremonies, or *pujas*, when the family gathers around a specific spacial center where a *puja* is being performed. This signifies how a natural articulation could develop between the practice of watching 'religious soap operas' and religious practices, in the redefinition of domestic sphere. This sphere has become increasingly central in redescribing how the family would interact with each other. Having lived both in a joint family and later in a nuclear family, I can remember the ways in which the television broadcast would be the site where conflicting family relations become normalized and smoothed over in the congregation of the entire family, in the space of the living room, and the sphere of the household, in exactly the same way a *puja* would do.

The central position of television in reshaping the domestic sphere and household space is also evident in the way in which the space and sphere is regulated by television. Particularly in terms of the variety of relationships between gender and age, the question of regulation of this sphere and space becomes crucial. For instance, within urban families one relation that is filled with contradictions and subordination is the one between the domestic servant and the other members of the household. This relation sees interesting changes in the redefined domestic space and sphere determined by television. While, in the absence of the medium, the servant might not be allowed within the private spaces of the bedroom (except perhaps to clean the room), television has opened up this space for unrestricted entry by the servant. Within the naturalized practice of watching television 'together,' the servant occupies almost equal

[14] For instance, in the urban context, a park, or tea shop, or even a temple would be the primary public space where leisure would be spent.

status when watching television. In fact, servants are often invited into private spaces to watch a program such as *Mahabharat*. Correspondingly, tensions are generated if servants are not permitted to enter that private sphere, particularly if a serial such as *Mahabharat* is being broadcast. This signifies the natural expectation that everybody should be allowed to participate in the practice of watching a 'religious soap opera' like *Mahabharat*—the quintessential Indian epic. In these ways, the internal contradictions within families and the distribution and regulation of space is becoming redefined.

Similarly, the notion of an 'outsider' in these spaces is also reshaped. By transporting leisure activities into the private spaces and spheres of the home, public relations are not necessarily broken. Thus friends who would have spent their leisure in the public sphere of a park or tea shop would now readily enter the unregulated private space of a living room or bedroom to continue the same socialization, now, however, around a rediscovered cultural center of a television serial.

In both senses of space and sphere, television has been able to reshape the way in which urban families now interact with television, to regulate and describe their private and public spaces. Television is considered a naturalized part of the everyday practices of the family. Placing the television set in the living room remains an invitation to redefine the space and the sphere where the family would interact, not only in watching a particular serial or news broadcast, but to resolve differences that are extra-textual. Indeed, the television text becomes the center around which contradictions are resolved. In this sense, watching television is now a central household practice which has not only redefined domestic space but also reshaped the domestic rhythm, use, distribution and regulation of household time.

The fact that television is able to redefine domestic time and the rhythm of domestic life has been discussed by researchers such as Bryce (1987) and Morley and Silverstone (1988). This redefinition of time is articulated with a variety of contradictions and the structuration within the family. As Morley and Silverstone point out:

What we begin to trace here is the interweaving of family time and broadcast time and the ways in which the two become intermeshed at the level of daily routines. Thus, we would suggest that the time boundaries of broadcasting, for instance in relation to the distinction between 'adult' and 'children's' viewing times, are often also enmeshed in the procedures through which age status is defined in the family (Morley and Silverstone, 1988).

This is precisely what happens in the Indian urban household too. There are a variety of relations that are produced around the status of women, children and servants within the domestic sphere. These relations are redefined by the introduction of the television medium within the household. For instance, the serial *Mahabharat* described a private household time, when all conflicts would be set aside, and all the members of the household, as well as outsiders, would redefine that time, on Sunday mornings, to congregate in front of the television set. Perhaps the only other practice that regulates time so well are *pujas*. For example, in my household, Thursday breakfast was always delayed to accommodate my mother's weekly *puja*. This was an unquestioned and uncontested reshaping of domestic time, just as the Sunday breakfast was delayed to accommodate the practice of watching *Mahabharat*.

Simultaneously, structured relations are reemphasized in the regulation of household time around broadcasting time. For instance, one concern that is predominant in urban households is the way in which television viewing practices would conflict with the time set aside for studying and children's homework. This is resolved in a variety of ways. Two common ways are regulating the children by not letting them watch television during the time set aside for studying, or by shutting off the television when the children are expected to study. In both instances, the centrality of the television viewing practice is reiterated. This practice is reproduced as one that is central in household practices, and by not watching television everybody is depriving themselves of a practice that is considered natural and desirable within everyday practices.

Broadcasting time has also been able to redefine the domestic rhythms within the private sphere of everyday life. Using Hall's notion of polychronic and monochronic viewing, Bryce's ethnographic research provides evidence that families in the West use television time as a mode around which family activities are planned and carried out. This is precisely what Altman also suggests in the way in which television, through the use of sound, is able to redefine the rhythm of family activities. In a similar way, within urban households in India, Doordarshan has been able to redefine the use and regulation of time by the family. For example, Sunday mornings were organized around the watching of *Mahabharat*. All family activities came to a standstill at the time of this serial, when the entire family gathered around the television set to watch Krishna come home on the small screen.[15] Similarly, specific family activities, like the family dinner, have now either moved out of the space of the dining room to the living room, or the time has been shifted to fit the nine'o'clock television serial into the scheduling of dinner. Time is differently regulated now, with servants completing their work, and partitioning their work around specific serials.

Doordarshan has thus been able to enter into the very fabric of India's everyday life. Beyond redefining the space, sphere and time within the privacy of everyday life, Doordarshan has been able to articulate its textual practices with a variety of other practices. Indeed, the characters of the serials have become palpable with extra-textual meaning, and their centrality in India's popular culture is expressed in the following example which describes the articulation of the soap opera *Hum Log* with a variety of other practices:

> The identification with the family shown was so complete that in their anxiety to know if Badki was going to marry Doctor Ashwini, shopkeepers downed shutters to hurry home to their sets. People got hold of Seema Bhargava (who played Badki) on the street and demanded to know why she would not marry the good doctor. She had to oblige. Vinod Nagpal as Basesar and Sushma Seth as Dadi [the affectionate term for grandmother] became indelible parts of the viewer's experience. When the serial finally folded up, an ad in the Delhi papers said against a picture of Sushma: 'We will miss you Dadi' (Das Gupta, 1990).

[15] Indeed, *Mahabharat* was able to redefine public time too. During the time the serial was broadcast nearly all activities came to a standstill as people would be glued to the screen. Public activities were scheduled around the serial, and taxis would be unavailable around that hour. I had the interesting experience of being hurtled through Calcutta in a taxi because the driver wanted to reach me to my destination, and then get to his friend's place to watch *Mahabharat*.

This is precisely what was repeated in the case of *Ramayan*, and later with *Mahabharat*. The articulation of the medium into the fabric of everyday life is indeed complete, and naturalized. The ideological struggle to find a space within the discourses and practices of everyday life has been successfully contested by Doordarshan, and it has become an indelible part of the everyday practices in India.

The significance of this outcome lies in the effectivity of the medium in reshaping a variety of other practices in India's everyday life. The textual strategies and characters of Doordarshan have now been mobilized into political action, where the Hindu-Hindi center is reproduced in the political campaigns of television stars such as Deepika (who played Sita in *Ramayan*) and other similar characters. Doordarshan has been able to implicate the way in which, at least the urban people, are rethinking their private space and time, and putting television in an increasingly central and natural position within their everyday activities. It is precisely for these reasons that it becomes important to rethink the practices that Doordarshan is reproducing as the dominant and natural practices of India's national image and popular culture.

## In Conclusion

I shall summarize the key aspects of this project. The underlying theoretical assumptions of this study emerged from the rich area of work often labelled 'cultural studies,' which is primarily embodied in the work of scholars at the Birmingham Center for Cultural studies. Cultural studies have now been incorporated within the tradition of communication studies in North America. Although the question of the origin and chronology of development of this tradition of research is contested, one issue that remains crucial is that the entire tradition of cultural studies emerged out of a Western way of thinking, engaged in researching the cultures of the West. However, in this project, this tradition of research has been used to understand Indian culture and its contradictions, focusing on the cultural formation of television. In this respect, I argue, that this study increases the scope of cultural criticism, as well as demonstrate that there is an epistemological advantage in rethinking television in India from the cultural studies perspective.

The primary goal of this project has been to conduct a textual analysis of a variety of texts on television, focusing particularly on the serial *Mahabharat*, to arrive at some indications of the role of television in India's popular culture. The assumption is that such an endeavor will provide a better understanding of the state of television in India and its relation to a broader set of elements in India's popular culture, and provide directions towards additional work that can be done to better understand the medium and its relation to India's popular culture.

The state controlled, non-autonomous institution of television in India developed significantly in the decade of the eighties. There have been significant improvements in technology, leading to the introduction of color on television and the increased accessibility of the medium to a large part of the Indian population. The National Network, emanating from the central broadcast facilities of New Delhi, now dominates the transmission schedule of television. This institution now reaches most of India, reshaping the nature of India's popular culture. This development has been marred with struggles, for instance, those around the unresolved question of autonomy and Doordarshan's focus on educational-entertainment. What has emerged is a technologically sophisticated medium which is still struggling to discover its legitimate role in India's popular culture. This struggle provided the rationale to embark on this project particularly because the current research on Doordarshan does not necessarily recognize this struggle, and fails to acknowledge the role of television as a cultural formation with its specific, non-guaranteed and provisional role in popular culture.

The underlying assumption about culture and popular culture, in this project, has been that culture is an ideological product of the articulation of a variety of practices. This moves culture away from any specific artefact and places it within the realm of practices and everyday life activities. This democratizes culture and frees it from the shackles of elitism, making it possible to speak of culture and popular culture interchangeably. This is the theoretical position that has emerged out of a rethinking of culture and cultural practices, particularly within the cultural studies context. Contradictory elements, in a conjunctural unity, produce popular culture at any moment in time. Given the non-essential nature of articulated unities, with no necessary correspondence between the elements, culture is open to ideological struggle. This struggle is over articulating a set of practices as the preferred cultural practices. These practices also represent the activities of particular social blocs who forge a position of hegemonic leadership by winning the consent of the other blocs. This hegemonic position is not with any guarantees and is open to ideological struggle. This position also articulates a set of practices as the natural and preferred practices that produce popular culture. In India, television—its representational practices and the practice of watching television—has been produced as a crucial element in this articulation.

Given the primacy of television in this articulated unity, it becomes useful to consider the text of television as a site where the struggles in the cultural arena are reproduced as struggles over meaning. This provides the possibility of textual analysis being a way of rethinking, deconstructing and demystifying these struggles. Textual analysis, which incorporates a deep critique of the primary text and the related secondary text, provides a point of departure to understand what ideological connections are made between the primary text and other elements of popular culture. However, prior to embarking on such a critique, it is important to identify a specific set of texts or genres which can be considered central in rethinking the position of television.

This argument provided the rationale for embarking on a brief genre analysis of Doordarshan, and examining the limits, boundaries, differences and similarities between the plethora of texts available on television. In doing this, a variety of genres were identified by using a semantic-syntactic approach to genre theory and history, where similar units and connections are identified in the texts to classify them into specific genres. This leads to the identification of 'religious soap operas' as a predominant genre on Doordarshan.

Among them, *Mahabharat* has been selected for deeper analysis. A close textual analysis of representative episodes of this serial indicates that a selected set of textual practices are able to circulate a preferred set of elements as the key elements in popular culture. The practices are articulated with a hegemony of a Hindi speaking, Hindu social bloc that represents a male hegemony located around northern India. The practices reproduced on the serial are also articulated with the increasing visibility of Hindu fundamentalists in the reshaping of the Indian image.

The issue of the 'Indian image' provides the opportunity to reexamine the notion of the nation. Working out of a historical perspective and then considering the internal contradictions in a nation, it is possible to rethink the nation as the articulation of a variety of contradictory practices where the practices of a dominant social bloc are represented as the national practices. Around these practices of a Hindu-Hindi hegemony, a national identity and a nation is imagined. Doordarshan, as a state controlled medium, is able to represent these practices as the national practices. Moreover, Doordarshan is able to articulate itself with the national practices thus reproducing and circulating a limited set of practices as the preferred practices of the Indian nation. These are the practices that reproduce the image of India as *bharat*, where the rule of *dharma*, as embodied in the *Mahabharat* and *Ramayan*, are reproduced as natural, unequivocal and preferred. This is articulated with the emerging Hindu reawakening, where the notion of a non-secular Hindu state is becoming increasingly predominant. Within this rethinking of India, the primary struggle is between Hindus and Muslims with which several other conflicts are now articulated. And it is the non-essential nature of articulated unities that provides the opportunity to demystify this conjunction and disarticulate the variety of struggles from the artificial primacy of religious differences. Doordarshan, through *Mahabharat* and *Ramayan*, has been able to circulate the primacy of this precise struggle between *dharma* and *adharma* as the struggle between Hindus and non-Hindus to recapture the lost glory of the Hindu *bharat* of the Pandavas and Ram.

Yet, Doordarshan is not free of internal contradictions. Indeed, the struggles over language, region, religion and gender are textually reproduced in the diversity of texts that are available on Doordarshan now. This opens up the possibility of ideological struggle where the hegemony of the leading bloc can be questioned, both in popular culture and in its representation on Doordarshan. This is precisely why it is important to question the emerging hegemony, when the space for struggle is still available.

Simultaneously, Doordarshan has captured a legitimate position in the everyday practices of India. Particularly within the urban blocs, television has how been accepted as a natural practice, well enmeshed within the domestic space and rhythm of everyday life. By mobilizing and articulating a variety of elements, television and all that encompasses it now implicates popular cultural, social and political practices. It is this mature medium that can now reshape Indian popular culture.

The hegemony that is embodied, reproduced and circulated on Doordarshan is also articulated with the political struggles in India now, manifest in the increasing secessionist movements, the emergence of communal disharmony and a move away from a secular ideology—in the image of a Hindu state. Doordarshan has been able to provide some voice to the marginalized, but that role is increasingly stifled in the growing conservatism of Hindu hegemony. In order to play a role in India's popular culture and retain the polysemy that is inherent in television, Doordarshan needs to continue this struggle and provide the site where the struggle can be played out and articulated with popular action.

The question of the audience has been largely bracketed out in this analysis. This remains yet another area of analysis that needs attention. It is necessary to engage in a reexamination of the audience to discover the variety of ways in which the television text is being negotiated for meaning. Given the diversity of the television audience in India, it is important to develop a set of frameworks to identify the various contradictory elements in the audience. The four vectors—language, region, religion and gender—can perhaps be the key modes along which the audience is structured. However, a deeper rethinking of the audience is needed to further legitimize and authenticate many of the conclusions that are elaborated here.

This lack—of bracketing out the audience—is precisely what many ethnographers have pointed out as the primary drawback of textual studies such as this one. Janice Radway (1984) has urged the textual critic to descend from the 'ivory tower' of academic criticism and enter the everyday life of the audience and reexamine the variety of ways in which television is articulated with the everyday practices of the viewer.

Nevertheless, a textual analysis such as this takes a step towards rethinking the issues that are often considered as normal and natural, pointing out that there are indeed contradictions that exist. These contradictions need to be examined, to take us a step forward in trying to understand 'what's going on.' In this instance, with Doordarshan and India's popular culture.

# Epilogue

After this work was completed, and while the manuscript was being readied for publication, certain events occurred in India that reflected some of the findings of the textual analysis of the *Mahabharat* television serial. The Hindu chauvinism that was produced around the religious serialized programs such as *Mahabharat* and *Ramayan* found ugly expression in December 1992 in the *karsevaks'* attack on the mosque at Ayodhya and the ensuing religious riots across the nation, particularly in Bombay and other urban areas.

These events underscore a popular cultural movement which marginalizes the Muslims of India and articulates the national image of the country with a Hindu ideology. Needless to say, within the conjunctural notion of society, these events need to be connected with other social, cultural and political elements in the popular culture, amongst which television plays a critical role. The turn of events at the end of 1992 reflect this growing popular cultural leaning towards finding a national image around the saffron color of Hinduism. This is no different from the reflection of the image of *bharat* portrayed over and over again in the religious soap operas of Doordarshan.

While Hindu chauvinism was raising its ugly head across the nation, there was another critical event taking place which was re-shaping the popular cultural map of India. This was the emergence and rapid growth of satellite and cable television in India. With the adaptation of grass-roots level cable technology, a burgeoning consumer economy, and abundance of privately produced programs in South Asia, satellite television programs such as Star TV and Music Television (MTV) gained a significant purchase on the Indian television audience. Doordarshan finally had a sizeable competition as more and more urban viewers opted for the privately produced cable programming.

These programs are also primarily produced outside India, in other parts of South Asia, and the fare includes Hindi and English programs, and a large range from Hindi feature films to American soap operas. The significance of this lies in the decreasing popularity of Doordarshan and the consequent dearticulation of the staple Doordarshan programs from the popular culture produced by television. Increasingly the secondary popular cultural text around television is concerned with MTV, CNN and Star TV, as the importance of Doordarshan programs declines. Consequently, the focus of future research needs to be on the new cultural map and national image produced by the globalization of television programming in India. Yet, this does not reduce the importance of the role that Doordarshan has played in the past three decades in producing the television culture in India. As with most things in everyday life, the emergence of cable and satellite programming will change and modify the cultural arena, but will not be able to erase the cultural memory of three decades of the state-controlled ideological state apparatus that Doordarshan has been.

*July 1993*

# Bibliography

**Advani, L.K.** (1990). Text of Speech Given at RSS Gathering. *The Telegraph*, 7, 17 May.

**Aghi, M.** (1979). The Effectiveness of Science Education Programming. *Journal of Communication*, 29, 4: 104–5.

**Agrawal, B.C.** (1978). *Satellite Instructional Television Experiment: Television Comes to Villages*. Bangalore, ISRO.

————. (1986). Television Studies in India: The State of the Art. Paper presented at the International Television Studies Conference, London, UK.

**Allen, R.C.** (1983). On Reading Soaps: A Semiotic Primer. In E.A. Kaplan (ed), *Regarding Television*. Los Angeles: American Film Institute/University Publications of America, pp. 97–108.

————. (1985). *Speaking of Soap Operas*. Chapel Hill: University of North Carolina Press.

————. (1987). Reader Oriented Criticism and Television. In R.C. Allen (ed), *Channels of Discourse*. Chapel Hill: The University of North Carolina Press, pp. 74–111.

**Althusser, L.** (1971). *Lenin and Philosophy and Other Essays*. New York: Monthly Review Press.

————. (1986). Ideology and Ideological state apparatuses. In G. Hanhardt (ed), *Video Culture*. Rochester: Visual Studies Workshop Inc., pp. 56–95.

**Altman, R.** (1986). Television/Sound. In T. Modelski (ed), *Studies in Entertainment: Critical Approaches to Mass Culture*. Bloomington and Indianapolis: Indiana University Press, pp. 39–54.

————. (1987). *The American Film Musical*. Bloomington: Indiana University Press.

**Amin, S.** (1980). *Class and Nation*. New York: Monthly Review Press.

**Anderson, B.** (1983). *Imagined Communities: Reflections on the Origin and Spread of Nationalism*. London: Verso.

**Ang, I.** (1985). *Watching Dallas*. London: Methuen.

**Apte, M.L.** (1978). Introduction. In M.L. Apte (ed), *Mass Culture, Language and Arts in India*. Bombay: Popular Prakashan, pp. 1–9.

**Astroff, R.J.** (1987). *Cultural Nationalism in the Age of Mass Media: Television and the Struggle Over Meaning in Wales*. Doctoral dissertation, University of Illinois, Urbana-Champaign.

**Badhwar, I.** (1991). The Mood: Anger and Anguish. *India Today*, 31 December, pp. 42–46.

**Barthes, R.** (1975). *S/Z*. London: Cape.

——————. (1977). An Introduction to the Structural Analysis of Narratives. In R. Barthes, *Image-Music-Text*, ed., and trans. S. Heath. London: Fontana.

**Bedi, B.** (1987). Doordarshan's Praiseworthy Workshop. *The Telegraph*, 20 June.

**Bennett, T.**, and **J. Woollacott**. (1987). *Bond and Beyond*. New York: Methuen.

**Bhanot, T.R.** (1990). *Mahabharat, Part 1*. New Delhi: Dreamland Publications.

**Bhargava, S.** (1987). Divine Sensation. *India Today, 12*, 8: 70–71.

**Bharucha, R.** (1983). *Rehearsals of Revolution: The Political Theater of Bengal*. Honolulu: University of Hawaii Press.

**Block, C., D.R. Foote**, and **J.K. Mayo**. (1979). SITE Unseen: Implications for Programming and Policy. *Journal of Communication, 29*, 4: 114–24.

**Brook, P. Brundson, C.**, and **D. Morley**. (1981). Everyday Television: Nationwide. In T. Bennett, S. Boyd-Bowman, C. Mercer, and J. Woollacott (eds), *Popular Television and Film*. London: British Film Institute, pp. 118–41.

**Bryce, J.W.** (1987). Family Time and Television Use. In T. Lindolf (ed), *Natural Audiences*. New York: Ablex, pp. 121–38.

**Buci-Glucksmann, C.** (1980). *Gramsci and the State*. London: Lawrence and Wishart.

**Bumiller, E.** (1990). *May You be the Mother of a Hundred Sons*. New York: Fawcett Columbine.

**Carnoy, M.** (1984). *The State and Political Theory*. Princeton: Princeton University Press.

**Chakravarty, S.** (1987). Identity and Authenticity: Nationhood and the Popular Indian Cinema 1947–62. Doctoral dissertation, University of Illinois.

**Chambers, I.** (1986). *Popular Culture: The Metropolitan Experience*. London: Methuen.

**Chanda Committee** (1966). *Chanda Committee Report*. Government of India: Ministry of Information and Broadcasting.

**Chandrasekhar, R.** (1982). *Aspects of Adult Education*. Madras: New Era Publications.

**Chaney, D.** (1986). A Symbolic Mirror of Ourselves: Civic Ritual in Mass society. In R. Collins, J. Curran, N. Granham. P. Scannell, P. Schlesinger and C. Sparks (eds), *Media, Culture and Society: A Critical Reader* (London: Sage, pp. 247–65.

**Chaudhuri, M.M.** (1986). India: From SITE to INSAT. *Media in Education and Development, 19*, 3: 134–40.

**Chowdhury, B.** (1987a). Films, Films and More Films. *The Telegraph*, 11, 23 May.

——————. (1987b). The Indispensability of Doordarshan. *The Telegraph*, 11, 6 June.

——————. (1987c). Censorship, Doordarshan Style. *The Telegraph*, 20 June.

——————. (1988). Calcutta's Second Channel: An Amazing Lack of Purpose. *The Telegraph*, 10, 15 January.

**Coldevin, G.C.** (1974). Educational Television Research in India. *Public Telecommunications Review*: 75–91.

**Coldevin, G.**, and **C. Amundsen** (1985). The Use of Communication Satellites for Distance Education: A World Perspective. *Canadian Journal of Educational Communication, 14*, 1: 4–5.

**D'Silva, A., H. Shetty**, and **A. Dev.** (1988). India's No. 1 TV Star. *TV and Video World, 5*, 7: 22–28.

Danheisser, P. (1975). The Satellite Instructional Television Experiment: The Trial Run. *Educational Broadcasting International, 8*, 4: 155–59.

Das Gupta, C. (1980). *Talking About Films*. New Delhi: Orient Longman.

——————. (1981). *The Cinema of Satyajit Ray*. New Delhi: Vikas.

——————. (1988). Turning Point—Hopefully. *The Telegraph*, 10.

——————. (1990). A Darshan not Door Enough. *The Telegraph*, 40–43

Davis, H.B. (1978). *Towards a Marxist Theory of Nationalism*. New York: Monthly Review Press.

Deutsch, K.W., and W.J. Foltz. (1966). *Nation Building*. New York: Atherton Press.

Dharker, A. (1987). On Hindi News. *TV and Video World 4*, 3: 25–28.

Dhawan, B.D. (1973). Economics of TV Software: What Makes Expansive. *The Economic Times*, 20 January.

Dimock, E.C. and D.Levertov. (1974). *In Praise of Krishna: Songs from Bengali*. Garden City: Doubleday and Co., Inc.

Dua, M.R. (1979). *Programming Potential of Indian Television*. New Delhi: Communication Publications.

Dumont, L. (1970). *Homo Hierarchicus*. London: Paladin Granada Publishing Ltd.

Eco, U. (1972). Towards a Semiotic Inquiry into the TV Message. *Working Papers in Cultural Studies*, 3: 103–26.

——————. (1976). *A Theory of Semiotics*. Bloomington: The Indiana University Press.

Elder, J.W. (1978). Mass Culture in Historical and Contemporary India. In M.L. Apte (ed), *Mass Culture, Language and Arts in India*. Bombay: Popular Prakashan, pp. 10–29.

Ellis, J. (1981). *Visible Fictions: Cinema: Television: Video*. London: Routledge.

Elsaesser, T. (1986). Tales of Sound and Fury: Observations on the Family Melodrama. In B.K. Grant (ed) *Film Genre Reader*. Austin: University of Texas Press, pp. 278–308.

——————. (1989). *New German Cinema: A History*. London: British Film Institute.

Eppan, K.E. (1979). The Cultural Component of SITE. *Journal of Communication, 29, 4*: 106–13.

Feuer, J. (1987). Genre Study and Television. In R.C. Allen (ed), *Channels of Discourse*. Chapel Hill: The University of North Carolina Press, pp. 113–32.

Fiske, J. (1987a). *Television Culture*. New York: Methuen.

——————. (1987b). British Cultural Studies and Television. In R.C. Allen (ed), *Channels of Discourse*. Chapel Hill: The University of North Carolina Press, pp. 74–111.

——————. (1989). *Understanding Popular Culture*. Boston: Unwin Hyman.

Fiske, J., and J. Hartley. (1978). *Reading Television*. London: Methuen.

Forgcas, D. (1988). *An Antonio Gramsci Reader*. New York: Schocken Books.

Frith, S. (1978). *Sound Effects: Youth, Leisure and the Politics of Rock*. London: Constable.

Geertz, C. (1973). *The Interpretation of Cultures*. New York: Basic Books Inc.

Gerbner, G. (1970). Cultural Indicators: The Case of Violence in Television Drama. *Annals of American Association of Political and Social Science*, 338: 69–81.

Ghosh, B. (1988). Doordarshan: Dawn Breaks Anew. *The Telegraph*, 10.

Gidwani, I. (1990). Letter from the Editor. *Upbeat*, 5, June.

Gilroy, P. (1986). Stepping Out of Babylon—Race, Class and Autonomy. In P. Gilroy and S. Hall (eds), *The Empire Strikes Back*. London: Methuen, pp. 276–314.

Gitlin, T. (1981). Media Sociology: The Dominant Paradigm. In J.C. Wilhoit and H. De Bock (eds), *Mass Communication Review Yearbook, Vol. 2*. Beverly Hills: Sage Publications, pp. 73–122.

Government of India, Ministry of Information and Broadcasting. (1966). *Radio and Television: Report of the Committee on Broadcasting and Information Media*. New Delhi: Publications Division.

Gramsci, A. (1971). *Selections from Prison Notebooks*. New York: International Publishers.

Grossberg, L. (1984). Strategies of Marxist Cultural Interpretation. *Critical Studies in Mass Communication*, 1: 392–421.

—————. (1986). History, Politics and Postmodernism: Stuart Hall and Cultural Studies. *Journal of Communication Inquiry*, *10*, 2: 61–75.

Hall, S. (1980a). Cultural Studies: Two Paradigms. *Media, Culture and Society*, 2: 57–72.

—————. (1980b). Encoding/Decoding. In S. Hall, D. Hobson, A. Lowe, and P. Willis (eds), *Culture, Media, Language*. London: Hutchinson, pp. 128–39.

—————. (1980c). Cultural Studies and the Centre: Some Problematics and Problems. In S. Hall, D. Hobson, A. Lowe and P. Willis (eds), *Culture Media, Language*. London: Hutchinson, pp. 15–47.

—————. (1985). Signification, Representation, Ideology: Althusser and the Post-Structuralist Debates. *Critical Studies in Mass Communication*, 2: 91–114.

—————. (1986a). On Postmodernism and Articulation. *Journal of Communication Inquiry*, *10*, 2: 45–60.

—————. (1986b). The Problem with Ideology—Marxism Without Guarantees. *Journal of Communication Inquiry*, *10*, 2: 28–44.

Hall, S., I. Connell and L. Curti. (1977). The 'Unity' of Current Affairs Television. *Working Papers in Cultural Studies*, 9. London: Hutchinson, pp. 51–94.

Hartmann, P., B.R. Patil and A. Dighe. (1989). *The Mass Media and Village Life: An Indian Study*. New Delhi: Sage Publications.

Hay, J. (1987a). *Popular Film Culture in Fascist Italy*. Bloomington: Indiana University Press.

—————. (1987b). Toward the Study of Television Formations in a Recombinant Culture. *Cultural Studies*: 377–82.

Hebdige, D. (1979). *Subculture: The Meaning of Style*. London: Methuen.

—————. (1981). Towards a Cartography of Taste. *Block*, 4.

Hoggart, R. (1957). *The Uses of Literacy*. London: Oxford University Press.

—————. (1969). Contemporary Cultural Studies. *Working Papers in Cultural Studies*. Birmingham, UK: Center for Contemporary Cultural Studies.

Jain, G.C. (1978). Low Cost Television Studio Equipment for Broadcast Applications in Developing Countries. *Educational Broadcasting International*, *11*, 1: 48–50.

Jaitley, A. (1991). Crossfire: Secularism. *India Today*, 15 May: 61–73.

Karnik, K. (1981). Developmental Television in India. *Educational Broadcasting International*, *14*, 3: 131–35.

Katz, E., and T. Liebes. (1987). Decoding Dallas: Notes from a Cross-Cultural Study. In H. Newcomb (ed), *Television: The Critical View*. New York: Oxford University Press, pp. 419–32.

King, R.D. (1986). The Language Issue Revisited. In J.R. Roach (ed), *India 2000: The Next Fifteen Years*. Riverdale: The Riverdale Company Inc. Publishers, pp. 135–45.

Kinsley, D.R. (1982). *Hinduism: A Cultural Perspective*. Englewood Cliffs: Prentice-Hall, Inc.

Kozloff, S.R. (1984). Narrative Theory and Television. In R.C. Allen (ed), *Channels of Discourse*. Chapel Hill: The University of North Carolina Press, pp. 42–73.

Krishnamoorthy, P.V. (1975). Learning Through Satellite Broadcasting. *Literacy Discussion*, 6, 3: 105–20.

Krishnaswamy, C. (1986). Indian Women and Television: A Study of the Woman Viewers of Madras. Paper presented at the International Television Studies Conference.

Kumar, K.J. (1986). Media Education: An Indian Perspective. Paper presented at the International Television Studies Conference.

Kuppuswamy B. (1976). *Communication and Social Development in India*. New Delhi: Sterling Publishers Pvt. Ltd.

Lerner, D. (1958). *The Passing of Traditional Society: Modernizing the Middle East*. New York: The Free Press.

Lerner, D. and Schramm W. (1967). *Communication and Change in Developing Countries*. Honolulu, Hawaii: East West Center Press.

Levi-Strauss, C. (1955). The Structural Study of Myth. *Journal of American Folklore*, LXXVIII, 270.

Lull, J. (ed). (1988). *World Families Watch Television*. Newbury Park: Sage.

Luthra, H.R. (1986). *Indian Broadcasting*. New Delhi: Publications Division, Ministry of Information and Broadcasting, Government of India.

Madhok, B. (1970). *The Rationale of the Hindu State*. Delhi: Indian Book Gallery.

Mathias, T A. (1975). Mass Education: Its Importance in India. *New Frontiers in Education*, 5, 8: 25–36.

Mathur J.C. (1978). The Use of Audio-Visual Media for the Education of Adults. *Indian Journal of Adult Education*, 39, 5–6: 35–40.

Mazumdar, S. (1990). Letter to the Editor. *The Telegraph*, 7, 9 June.

Menon, N. (1986). Traditional Culture, New Mediums, Interaction, and Diffusion. In J.R. Roach (ed), *India 2000: The Next Fifteen Years*. Riverdale: The Riverdale Company Inc. Publishers, pp. 27–41.

Miller, B.S. (1986). *The Bhagavad Gita: Krishna's Counsel in Times of War*. London: Bantam Books Inc.

Minault, G. (1986). Women in Contemporary India: The Quest for Equal Participation and Justice. In J.R. Roach (ed), *India 2000: The Next Fifteen Years*. Riverdale: The Riverdale Company Inc. Publishers, pp. 215–28.

Mirchandani, G.C. (1976). *India Backgrounders—Television in India*. New Delhi: Vikrant Press.

Mitra, A. (1988a). Interconnections and Cross-Overs between Film and Television in India. Paper presented at the Ohio University Film Conference.

—————. (1988b). Significance of Genres on Indian Television. Paper presented at the International Television Studies Conference.

Mody, B. (1976). Towards Formative Research in TV for Development. *Educational Broadcasting International, 9,* 4: 160–63.

————. (1978). Lessons from the Indian Satellite Experiment. *Educational Broadcasting International, 11,* 3: 117–20.

————. (1979). Programming for SITE. *Journal of Communication, 29,* 4: 90–98.

Moores. S. (1988). The Box on the Dresser: Memories of Early Radio. *Media, Culture and Society, 10.*

Morley, D. (1980). *The Nationwide Audience: Structure and Decoding.* London: British Film Institute.

Morley, D., and R. Silverstone. (1988). Domestic Communication—Technologies and Meaning. Paper presented at the International Television Studies Conference.

Mulay, V. (1978). The Teacher in the Sky. *Prospects: Quarterly Review of Education, 8,* 4: 531–34.

Naqvi, S. (1990). A Muslim's Response to L.K. Advani. *The Telegraph,* 7, 26 May.

Neale, S. (1981). Genre and Cinema. In T. Bennett, S. Boyd-Bowman, C. Mercer, J. Woollacott (eds), *Popular Television and Film.* London: British Film Institute, pp. 6–15.

————. (1990). Question of Genre. *Screen, 31,* 1: 45–66.

Newcomb, H. (1987). Texas: A Giant State of Mind. In H. Newcomb (ed), *Television: The Critical View.* New York: Oxford University Press, pp. 221–28.

Noorani, H. (1978). Children and Television in India. *Phaedrus, 5,* 1: 34–36.

Norwood, F. (1978). Broadcast Satellite: Appropriate Technology Available Now. *International Educational and Cultural Exchange, 13,* 3: 27–28.

O'Sullivan, T., J. Hartley and D. Saunders. (1983). *Key Concepts in Communication.* New York: Methuen.

Padamsee, A. (1987). What is 'News'? *TV and Video World, 4,* 5: 64–65.

Pai A. (1988). *Amar Chitra Katha: Tales of the Mahabharat.* Bombay: India Book House.

Pecheux, M. (1982). *Language, Semantics and Ideology.* New York: St. Martin.

Propp, V. (1968). *The Morphology of the Folktale.* Austin: University of Texas Press.

Radway, J. (1984). Interpretive Communities and Variable Literacies: The Function of Romance Reading. *Daedalus, 113*: 49–73.

Rahman, M. (1987). Casting a Spell, *India Today, 12,* 4: 48–50.

Rahman, S. (1974). Technology and Communication: An Indian Experience. *ASPBAE Journal, 9,* 1: 65–73.

Rajagopalachari, C. (1989). *Mahabharata.* Bombay: Bharatiya Vidya Bhawan.

Reddi, U.V. (1987). Television in Higher Education: The Indian Experience. *Media in Education and Development, 20,* 4: 128–33.

Rehman, S. (1979). Communication Technology for Adult Education. *Indian Journal of Adult Education, 40,* 12: 13–18.

Sainath, P. (1990). The Sponsor's Power over Doordarshan. *The Telegraph,* 5, 5 June.

Sarabhai, K.V. (1985). Strategy for Environmental Education: A Strategy for India. Paper presented at the Annual Meeting of the North American Association for Environmental Education.

Sarin, R. (1987). The Soap Opera of the Gods. *Sunday*, 11 April.
Sarkar, K. (1975). *Indian Cinema today: An Analysis*. New Delhi: Sterling Publishers Pvt. Ltd.
Sawhney, K. (1991). Mujra: New Respectability. *India Today*, 15 March: 82–84.
Schatz, T. (1981). *Hollywood Genres*. New York: Random House.
Seiter, E. (1987). Semiotics and Television. In R.C. Allen (ed), *Channels of Discourse*. Chapel Hill: The University of North Carolina Press, pp. 17–41.
Sengupta, S. (1990). Revealing Shots, Telling Clips. *The Telegraph*, 8, 9 June.
————. (1990). Rising to the Occasion. *The Telegraph*, 10, 15 May.
Shafer, B.C. (1955). *Nationalism: Myth and Reality*. New York: Harcourt, Brace and World Inc.
Sharma, K.L. (1986). *Caste, Class and Social Movements*. Jaipur: Rawat Publications.
Sharma, M. (1985). Distance Education. Professional Staff Paper. Manila: Asian Development Bank.
Sherring, M.A. (1974). *Hindu Castes and Tribes*. Delhi: Cosmo Publications.
Shukla, S. (1979). The Impact of SITE on Primary School Children. *Journal of Communication*, 29, 4: 99–103.
Silj, A. (1988). *East of Dallas*. London: British Film Institute.
Singh, A. (1984). Distance, Learning: From Correspondence Institutes to Open University via Distance Education Center. Paper presented at the All India Conference of Vice-Chancellors.
Singh, I.B. (1975). The Indian Mass Media System: Before, During and After the National Emergency.
Singh K. (1991). Crossfire: Secularism. *India Today*, 15 May: 61–73.
Singhal, A., J.K. Doshi and E. Rogers. (1988). The Diffusion of Television in India. Paper presented at the International Communication Association Conference.
Singhal, A., and E. Rogers. (1987). Television Soap Operas for Development in India. Paper presented at the International Communication Association Conference.
Solomos, J., B. Findlay, J. Jones and P. Gilroy. (1986). The Organic Crisis in British Capitalism and Race. In *The Empire Strikes Back*. London: Methuen, pp. 9–46.
Srinivas, M.N. (1962). *Caste in Modern India*. Bombay: Asia Publishing House.
Staff. (1987a). *Buniyaad*: After the Curtain Falls. *The Telegraph*, 11, 7 June.
————. (1987b). Educational TV Foundation Soon. *The Telegraph*, 12, 24 June.
————. (1987c). TV Guide. *TV and Video World*, 4, 3.
————. (1987d). A Pagan Sacrifice. *India Today, 12*, 19: 58–61.
———— (1988). How Accurate are TV Ratings? *The Telegraph*, 10, 16 June.
————. (1991). Poll Stars. *India Today* 15 May: 77.
Stam, R. (1983). Television News and its Spectator. In E.A. Kaplan (ed), *Regarding Television*. Los Angeles: American Film Institute/University Publications of America, pp. 97–108.
Todorov, T. (1977). *The Poetics of Prose*. Oxford: Blackwell.
Turner, G. (1988). *Film as Social Practice*. London: Routledge.

Verghese, B.G. (1981). A Philosophy for Development Communication: The View from India. *Media Asia*.

Volosinov, V. (1973). *Marxism and the Philosophy of Language*. New York: Seminar Press.

Weiner, M. (1986). India's Minorities: Who are They? What do They Want? In J.R. Roach (ed), *India 2000: The Next Fifteen Years*. Riverdale: The Riverdale Company Inc. Publishers, pp. 99–135.

Williams R., (1961). *The Long Revolution*. London: Chatto and Windus.

————. (1977). *Marxism and Literature*. Oxford: Oxford University Press.

Willis, P. (1977). *Learning to Labor*. London: Hutchinson.

Yechuri, S. (1991). Crossfire: Secularism. *India Today*, 15 May: 61–73.

# Index